Music From the Lake
And Other Essays

Also by Catharine Savage Brosman

POETRY
Watering (1972)
Abiding Winter (1983) [chapbook]
Journeying From Canyon de Chelly (1990)
Passages (1996)
The Swimmer and Other Poems (2000) [chapbook].
Places in Mind (2000)
Petroglyphs: Poems and Prose (2003) [chapbook].
The Muscled Truce (2003)
Range of Light (2007)
Breakwater (2009)
Trees in a Park (2010) [chapbook]
Under the Pergola (2011)
On the North Slope (2012)
On the Old Plaza (2014)

CREATIVE PROSE
The Shimmering Maya and Other Essays (1994)
Finding Higher Ground: A Life of Travels (2003)

CRITICISM
André Gide: l'évolution de sa pensée religieuse (1962)
Malraux, Sartre, and Aragon as Political Novelists (1964)
Roger Martin du Gard (1968)
Jean-Paul Sartre (1983)
Jules Roy (1988)
Art as Testimony: The Work of Jules Roy (1989)
An Annotated Bibliography of Criticism on André Gide, 1973-1988 (1990)
Dictionary of Literary Biography, vols. 65, 72, 83, 119, 123, edited (1988-1992)
Simone de Beauvoir Revisited (1991)
Twentieth-Century French Culture, 1900-1975, edited with an introduction (1995)
Retour aux Nourritures terrestres, edited, with David H. Walker (1997)
Visions of War in France: Fiction, Art, Ideology (1999)
Existential Fiction (2000)
Albert Camus (2000)
Louisiana Creole Literature: A Historical Study (2013)
Southwestern Women Writers and the Vision of Goodness (2016)

Music From the Lake
And Other Essays

by Catharine Savage Brosman

Chronicles Press
Rockford, Illinois
2017

Acknowledgments

Grateful acknowledgment is made to the publishers of the magazines and journals in which the following essays first appeared: *Chronicles: A Magazine of American Culture*: "The APA: Sanctioning the Sexual Abuse of Children," "How the Historical Novel Has Changed!", "In Defence of Poesie," "*The New Yorker* Under the Glass," "O Literature, Thou Art Sick," "Secure of Private Right," "The Uses of a Liberal Education"; *Sewanee Review*: "Four Modes of Book Collecting," "Islands of Our Years," "Literature and Its Contents"; *South Carolina Review*: "Generations," "In the Abbey." It is appropriate also to thank the Jambalaya Writers' Conference, Terrebonne Parish Library, Louisiana, for inviting me in 2014 to give the talk titled "What Are Poems Made Of?"

ISBN 978-1-943218-02-8

CONTENTS

Music From the Lake
And Other Essays

Preface

WITH CONSIDERABLE OVERLAPPING OF MODES, the writing in this collection is of three types. The opening and closing essays and certain others are memoirs, laced with reflections. Considerations on the principles and practice of literature, especially poetry, as well as my cultivation of it, and, more broadly, its place in culture and in our lives constitute another principal vein. The third variety is social and cultural commentary. In several essays, these types are woven together. The commentary is less foreign to the rest than might be supposed, for one of the arguments of the collection is that an aspect of poetry, as of personal life, is morality, to which social questions are, or should be, connected. (The eminent poet and novelist David R. Slavitt uses the phrase "the morality of vision.") The digressions contained herein, not infrequent, belong to "the very nature of our treatise," as Denis Diderot wrote in his *Lettre sur les aveugles.* Despite many parentheses and certain wanderings, however, these essays do not comprise what one anonymous reviewer, in summarizing Paul Auster's *Winter Journal*, called "loosely organized fragments."

Among the topics that arise are family roots and other human connections; places; travel; books; food; manners and morals; urban design; womanhood; liberal education; natural scenes and objects; and music and architecture. Directed toward discriminating readers, the volume as a whole may be taken as an exercise in seeing the world, even feeling it, and in assessing and appreciating experience (the author's, others', and one's own) and the power of literature to render it. Most of these pages date from the second decade of the present century. "Literature and Its Contents" belongs to the mid-1990's, when I lived in New Orleans; it and "Bright Field" contain references to that city and to my teaching at Tulane University.

My thanks go to my wonderful husband, Patric Savage, whose love, companionship, and unfailing support are priceless.

Music From the Lake

WHEN I WAS A GIRL, my bedroom was in a corner of the modest bungalow where I lived with my parents, in Denver. The casement windows, facing north and west, were so high that my view was only "the little tent of blue / which prisoners call the sky"—with a few tree boughs visible on the north side. When I lay in bed ill, I looked up as through skylights. Were they "magic" casements? Unlike those of John Keats, they certainly opened onto no foam, no sea, perilous or not. (Though sometimes I stood in tears, like Ruth amid the alien corn, feeling the world around me—despite the loving care of my good parents—to be utterly foreign.) But perhaps the panes and the sky beyond, whether blue or, as so often, gray or snowy white, did propose an idea of "faery lands." After all, I was a child (an only child, a product of the Depression), with a mighty, if controlled, imagination. Out there in the blue, was there not the untested, presumably unlimited, arena of action—the stage, as well as the stuff, of life? To project time onto space—a continuum, as it were—was simple; it was an existential *turning-toward*—toward the future that growth (the child's law) implied, a form of *élan vital.* Hemmed in, limited visions can reveal more than unframed; though the vastness of the ocean is felt better on the deck of a ship, a porthole gives a more concentrated sense of its presence. Think of the deepening effect of frames in paintings by Henri Matisse.

In the summer and other mild months, the casements could be opened; and since members of my parents' generation believed that fresh air was indispensable, often there were pleasant breezes and birdsong coming in at morning and evening, and late shadows of the branches could dance on the walls unmarked by the grid of panes. But my father feared the cold, rightly so, since he was not strong and was given to lung infections. (There had been tuberculosis in his family, and I was tested regularly.) Thus, in winter, the casements in my room, like the window in my parents' bedroom, remained shut. Such warm air as there was had to be husbanded. Until my paternal grandmother paid for conversion of the basement furnace to natural gas, it burned coal and had to be stoked—a heavy task and a cold one in the mornings. (My grandmother, who was born in Quebec in 1864 and had come to Colorado for her health, could underwrite the conversion because she had her own bank account—rare for a married woman of her generation—and spent as she saw fit, though never, I daresay, foolishly. She also traveled, going to Montreal or elsewhere with my aunts; or my grandparents traveled together. As readers will learn later, the traveling gene is strong in my family.)

Even with gas and a thermostat, however, the temperature in my parents' house was kept on the low side. My father tried later to flee the cold, with a wintertime stay in Arizona, then a year in South Texas, and, four years later, Texas again, where my parents remained for most of their final years. Yet strangely—in an atavistic move?—in the 60's my father arranged to go to England for a year; he and Mother lived through the coldest winter in decades, and for months he carried coal up the hill for a meager fire.

In the matter of the windows, he was clever, devising a way to admit fresh air in small quantities, while keeping the casements closed. He had a workman drill in one lower frame four holes the size of a half-dollar, fitted with a sliding cover. On milder winter days and nights, all four holes were bared; on harsh ones, with wind and low temperatures, only one or two.

Consequently, during the wintertime, outdoor sounds penetrated my room even less than sights did. And it was in winter, when sounds might be muffled by snow and one would expect few at night anyway, that I most wanted to listen. For we lived very close to Washington Park, which had, at its near end, a small lake and a picnic pavilion; and, when the lake was frozen over, as was usual in the cold months, skaters were often out in the evenings—late, it seemed to me—circling to a background of recorded music played over loudspeakers. Thus, through holes in the window frame I heard, even if faintly and unevenly, "The Skaters' Waltz" and other pieces, sounding through the neighborhood. Despite the popular setting, all the music was, I believe, from the standard repertory; it bore no resemblance to what is generally called "music" today. (This very week, as I write this from our summer place in Colorado Springs, I've been beset by sounds—noise, rather—from a "concert" in Acacia Park, an attractive downtown square with old trees, but made unappealing much of the time by sanctioned and unsanctioned audio happenings greatly amplified.) Perhaps, in Washington Park, portions of the "Swan Lake" score were played also; I pictured the girls in short skating skirts, suggestive of ballet dancers. I strained to hear more; I imagined myself out on the ice, bundled as hockey players are now (no tutus for me), laughing, tracing circles and figure eights, as if to trace eternity . . .

Eventually, I did learn to skate on ice, but in my earlier girlhood, for reasons unclear to me now—perhaps caution (two broken arms, the result of tomboy activities, made a conservative policy attractive for my parents); perhaps because we couldn't afford skates—I was not allowed to try. And I was *never* permitted to stay up late. Nor, in summer, was I ever allowed to swim—that is, dip into the water of the lake. We had picnics there sometimes, and my father occasionally rented a boat and rowed us out. Further contact with the water was forbidden, since those were the years of the polio epidemic. Only once as a girl was I in a pool—some visit to the YWCA arranged for the Girl Scout troop. Its waters were, supposedly, purified (they stank and were murky, as I remember); even so, my father was not happy that I'd been exposed to possible contagion.

All that prudence and thrift! (That is to say, wisdom.) "Attractive but dangerous": Such, I was told, were the lake and many other things besides. Danger had no appeal for me, nor, I believe, for others in my circle. For me, no tea or coffee either. (They might impede growth.) I had to swallow vitamins and supplements (needed especially because of wartime rationing), and there were repeated attempts to get more food down me—hot cereal in the morning, for example. We had no carbonated drinks in the house, though at age ten, on our first trip to Texas, I was given a Dr. Pepper. Later, after we left Colorado permanently for the Big Bend, we had cola or 7 Up in the lengthy, 100-degree afternoons. I first drank tea there when we were invited to someone's home; the hostess passed me a cup, and my mother allowed me to accept it. That was at age 16!

As I say, what caution—and what docility on my part! An adolescent now would be mocked—no, scorned and humiliated—if such innocence, worse than Candide's, were exposed. That ingenuousness is simply one face of the regularity and obedience displayed in films and television programs concerning family life at mid-century (the "Eisenhower years")—a stability, homogeneity, and order once viewed as the norm, now widely mocked by radical feminists and other cultural critics who think, apparently, that such a life and such a social arrangement, orderly and "patriarchal," were not only monotonous but oppressive and damaging for our little psyches. It is true that, unlike many who have come later, we did not cultivate rebellion and "transgress boundaries" in order to "find ourselves." James Dean was James Dean, not most of us. (A commentator writing about *The New York Times Book Review* of recent years concluded that "the editorial theme of the magazine—what it looks for in its reviewers and the books they like—is praise of transgression.")

Hasn't that mode of youthful training—the order, the orders—served me well my entire life, in the form of regular habits, self-discipline, avoidance of danger, and marvelously good health? What good cards in my hand! Such a life is not narrow or curmudgeonly either—just rational, like that of many friends. And it does not exclude a poetic dimension, notwithstanding what might be supposed by those familiar with modern poetry and poets' lives in many centuries. Poetry is the beautiful ordering of language. Didn't Wallace Stevens write in "The Idea of Order at Key West" of the "blessed rage for order"? Regarding the sort of regularity I allude to here, critics would speak of "inhibitions," which today's invasive child specialists and "liberators" damn in the name of all their idols, and critics would pronounce fatal to art, not recognizing that, as André Gide knew and wrote, art lives on constraint and dies from freedom.

Good health now notwithstanding, as a child I had, like my father, many colds, and they required confinement in bed (where the thought of the young Robert Louis Stevenson kept me company, as I likewise lay propped up on a pillow, two sometimes). Going to school then, even leaving the house for a minute, was out of the question. Congestion in the chest meant repeated application of camphor oil to the throat and chest and then having old pieces of flannel or Turkish toweling pinned to my pajama top. If the congestion was truly stubborn, my father rigged up a vaporizer, attached (I believe) to a light-bulb socket. The vaporizer contained some product whose unpleasant fumes, released by heat, wafted through the air and, supposedly, into my lungs. (Recalling this odor is not a Proustian moment.) When I was ill in winter 1942, my cousin Beth Bradshaw, much older—a surgical nurse in the Army—brought me a small planter in the shape of a fawn, with a bit of ivy sprouting from its back. On one occasion Mother, Father, and I all had influenza—the real one—and someone had to be hired to care for us. The person proclaimed herself a countess. In those years, during and after World War II, there surely were a few aristocrats floating around in need of employment; more to the point, anyone could proclaim herself one if she had a bit of an accent.

Despite what this caution might indicate, my parents attempted to make a normal child out of me. Unlike those millions now who believe their children unusually gifted and thus try to create an exceptional childhood for them, my parents agreed with countless others, of their time and before, who thought that the training of children should prepare them to be unremarkable adults—surely the great majority—and accept, or achieve, ordinary contentment. The novelist Roger Martin du Gard, who was awarded the Nobel Prize in 1937 and was, though a "bourgeois," by no means an ordinary person in his character, mind, and gifts, endeavored, he wrote, to provide a normal childhood for his daughter, Christine; if she was gifted, he said, that would become clear soon enough, but in the meantime she should be brought up like other French children, not steered toward nonconformity. (That there are notable and well-founded exceptions, such as Leopold Mozart and his son, does not invalidate the principle.)

I played outdoors with neighborhood friends, visited the Eugene Field branch library in Washington Park and played tennis on the courts there, attended Sunday School and Vacation Bible School, sometimes two in a summer. (My cousin Pat Michels, of Colorado Springs, the late-born daughter of Beth, the surgical nurse, remarked that she and her siblings were sent "to every Vacation Bible School on the West Side.") I was active in the same Girl Scout troop for years, went to the Scout camp in the Pike National Forest for five summers in a row, had music lessons (piano from my Aunt Mary on her Steinway, and flute and music theory from a teacher who had to give afternoon lessons to keep his family fed), spent time with my grandparents, aunts, and cousins, loved excursions to the mountains with any family that would take me, and of course went to school except for the winter in Arizona. The summer I turned 15—shortly before we left Colorado for good—I was allowed not only to attend summer school in a high school miles away but to ride my bike there. Traffic conditions in Denver streets were, to be sure, different from what they are now, when you're in danger even in a large land cruiser or a Yukon. Later that same year, down in Alpine, in the Big Bend, Texas law allowed me to learn to drive.

The bike had been sold by then, but I kept the tennis racket, although there were no municipal courts in that little town. Scout days were over; a last camp experience took place at a Methodist camp in the New Mexico mountains. It is scarcely necessary to add that there was no skating around either, although winters in the West Texas mountains are not mild. What would one have done for ice? The creek was dry, its bed hard sand and dust, except for summer gully-washers from time to time. There was no school or municipal natatorium either; I did not learn to swim until I reached the university. Nor did music fill the night air of the town. My poor father, turning on the radio in vain hopes of getting something other than country songs, used to sigh and ask, "Just a little Mozart, if you please, perhaps *Eine Kleine Nachtmusik*." I had my flute, however, and my voice, and did just about everything musical that the little town allowed. A year or so later, I won a music scholarship to the school in El Paso called Texas Western, formerly the School of Mines—now UTEP. I declined that offer, however, in order to attend what was then The Rice Institute.

There, I had my flute but participated in no musical activity; I was engaged in intellectual and writing pursuits. Anyhow, living a mile or so from campus and without a car, how could I, practically, attend evening rehearsals (during the daytime we went to classes and labs and otherwise were in the library) and then get home safely and in a timely fashion? I had no desire to stay up late; restrictions in my childhood had led to sensible habits. But, over the years, what music I have heard: on 78s, 45s, LPs, tapes, CDs, on radio, in concert hall, opera house, chamber-music hall, in church naves and choir stalls (sometimes I was a participant), and in parlors—even now in those few homes where not only is there a piano but it is still used. One February we attended a concert held at dusk in a glassy penthouse on the 40th floor of the high-rise where we live in Houston. The concert was presented by a 30-piece amateur symphony orchestra. Food and wine were available afterward in a serving area off the main room. As the players began the opening piece, Ottorino Respighi's "Ancient Airs and Dances," a silver-toned medevac helicopter en route to the Hermann Hospital pad flew by, its colored lights glowing, its lovely modernity contrasting (by sound as well as sight) with Respighi's retro music.

I do not recall having heard "The Skaters' Waltz" very often. It is not serious enough for the usual symphony orchestra program. As for "Swan Lake," of course one hears it often in recordings on classical-music stations and sees the ballet performed on arts television and by some ballet companies. The last performance I saw was memorable, certainly, but no frozen lake was nearby: It was at an estate outside of Florence, in July, in a fine outdoor setting above the lower Tuscan hills. Still, I could think of the winter hills of Colorado, of white skirts whirling with the skaters' movements and the wind.

And what about *Lohengrin*? I think the hero's boat does not arrive on a frozen stream. But, one thing leading to another, the swan which draws the boat bringing the medieval Germanic hero to the shore—accompanied by the sublime music of Richard Wagner—somehow has become conflated for me with Peter Ilyich Tchaikovsky's ballet and, more remotely (in my lifetime), with music on the lake in Washington Park. That Lohengrin forbade his lady to ask his origins makes the connection particularly apt. As medieval wisdom had it, we children of mystery who find ourselves here (as children, and, if we are lucky, subsequently as older human beings) must not inquire nor seek to see too much—neither about where we come from, who we are, nor where we are going, to borrow Paul Gauguin's phrasing of the great questions of being, painted onto his famous tri-panel work, done just before he attempted to kill himself (1897). Job likewise was told not to inquire, nor challenge what was; where was he when the foundations of the world were laid? Consider what happened to Oedipus and the parents of Oedipus; to Orpheus, when he turned to look at his beloved; to Psyche also; to Hamlet; and, worlds and times away, to certain characters of William Faulkner.

What, it may be asked, of the "bright immensities" of sky that a hymn evokes, and of the future I imagined through the casements—did they keep their promises? Very much so. I would not speak as in John Dryden's

Aureng-Zebe: "When I consider life, 'tis all a cheat." (It is impossible, however, to forget how many contemporaries did not find much fulfillment. Many died horrible deaths brought on by institutionalized evil.) For me, at least, much that was implicit has been fulfilled. Happiness surely comprises the chance to follow the law of one's own nature. That I became a writer was no wonder; I was a writer born. That I became a French professor was a choice, an excellent one, among other endeavors to which I might have devoted my life—history, English literature, or perhaps Spanish or music had I attended another university. (Rice had no such majors.) Not everything was faery land, though. A few nasty surprises attend upon being a woman, just as, in Occidental societies at least, there are burdens built into being a man. Did not the knights of yore, however, likewise make discoveries they could well have done without as they pursued their quests, the greatest being the quest for salvation?

I look back on my mother in this connection, as she moved into girlhood, then womanhood. She was born at the end of the 19th century. After graduating from Colorado Springs High School, where she studied, among other subjects, German, she taught school at Fountain, just a few miles away. She later put herself through what was then Colorado State Teachers' College in Greeley, and subsequently taught school, boarding with families, in two Wyoming towns, then in Denver. She worked in the summer on a dude ranch, not assisting the guests but teaching the owners' feebleminded daughter, who learned to read and write, in a childish way. In the early 30's, after both her parents had died, Mother went to the University of Chicago for a master's degree in child psychology. I think of the duties she had assumed during her young years and the adjustments she was obliged to make. She had helped care for a blind grandmother, then her elder sister's children, then her ill and dying parents. (And some feminists speak and write as if they alone had ever worked!) Finally she took on the duties of marriage, when she was well into middle age and thought she would never marry; then there was a child, perhaps a surprise. She stayed at home in my early years, but eventually, to help my father, who took several leaves, taught rather rowdy junior-high-school boys at the Colorado Military School—not a plum job—and, earlier and later, taught at Texas high schools. My grandmother, for all her independent mind, likewise had accepted her part in the drama, as wife and mother. (It is pertinent that she thought women should stay out of politics, believing it did not become them nor the body politic, and not being duped by the notion that peace would be achieved if only women ruled.)

Today's feminists focus on such things as percentages of women in jobs formerly the domain of men, promotions, salaries, sexual slurs in offices, various perceived "rights," and lesbian, transgendered, and single-parent issues. The most extreme among these self-appointed champions of reform campaign in favor of overturning nearly every civilized institution and tradition, even nature itself. Their obsessions have changed the social milieu and altered expectations; think of the measures that have been taken to accommodate women's demands! While of import to those particular women involved, and having various broad consequences, such concerns and any modifications that spring from them do not, however, touch on the essence of the feminine condition—that is, the particular nature of womanhood. True, the female nature can be denied or evaded, even altered by modern "physic," surgery, and behavior (as happens with compulsive athletes). Those who wish can, presumably, make themselves into warriors of a sort, though it is entirely against women's nature and they cannot be so effective as their male counterparts. (I allude not merely to measures of physical strength and endurance.) What happens to the core of the woman then I do not know, nor wish to know. Nature—in its ontological dimensions—remains with us, in any case, beyond any human notion such as "social construct."

The great Colorado sky, stormy earlier this afternoon, clears and evens out to dusky blue. I gaze across the peaks and picture their high recesses, their secrets. On a glacial tarn, swans of thought glide on the glassy, glistening surface. The music from the lake, the promises of the casements of long ago were no illusion, still less a vile prevarication like the lies we are served up now, shamelessly. Though I do not forget the wisdom of the Greeks, who said we should count no man happy until he dies, a smooth feeling, the lightest of silk cloaks, falls over the evening, and over me. On the lake of memory I see the graceful movements of the skaters, and hear the measures of the music, in sine waves of sound, through the holes in time.

Generations

i

Today, the 25th of January, is the natal anniversary of my aunt Flora Kathleen Hill. Born in 1900, she was usually as old as the century. At her birth, Queen Victoria, whose predecessor had died in 1837, was still on the throne. Aunt Flora was the fourth of six children, all born in Denver; only my father and uncle Jack were not Victorian babies. My grandparents were born in 1863 and 1864, respectively. To my grandmother, Phoebe, née Elliott, the monarch was important; as a Canadian (Scots-Irish), she was a British subject. Both Edward Hill, who had gone to Colorado from Illinois and studied medicine, and Phoebe, the independent woman I have just sketched, who went there for her health, lived well into old age, and they provided to me and my cousins not only outstanding models of character and intellect but, through their memories, acquaintance with earlier times in the United States and the Dominion of Canada. Edward was the descendant of a Hill who had arrived in America before the Revolution; Phoebe's family had arrived in Quebec from County Clare by the 1820's, if not earlier.

As for my mother, she and all her siblings were children of the 1880's or 1890's. Her parents, Arthur and Susan Stanforth, were born a few years after mid-century. Susan's older sister, Margaret Hawley, née Wright, married but childless, was born in either 1849 or 1852; the evidence is contradictory. I remember her well, since she lived until 1946. During the hard years of the War Between the States, she carded wool from the family sheep, it is said, and made lace to sell. Their father, Thomas, who had lost his first wife, had remarried; Margaret and Susan Wright were the children of this second marriage. At the time he remarried, he was near 50 years of age, having been born in Virginia in 1799, under the presidency of John Adams. Thus I need go back only three generations to reach the 18th century.

I have sketched how Mother, who was born in Colorado after her parents moved west from Missouri and Kansas, married late. Three of my first cousins were more than 20 years older than I; my daughter and a cousin of the same generation are 38 years apart. Mother did not know her maternal grandfather, Thomas, nor his wife, Sarilda (nor did I know mine), nor her paternal grandfather, born in 1813; but she knew her paternal grandmother,

Susanna, née Van Pelt. Ancestral connections with the Van Pelts go back to the 1660's in New Amsterdam. The long leaps from one generation to the next, owing to genes and improved medical care as well as personal choices and circumstantial and social causes, have existential effects. For me, the 19th century has almost the vitality of recent decades; I think of myself as the descendant of Mother's pioneer forebears and the granddaughter of Edward Hill and Phoebe Elliott. (My daughter's middle name is Elliott.) I have done countless things my grandmother did not do, and not a few that she would not approve of, were she alive; but, half-Victorian, I've still got certain attitudes of hers, among them the prejudice, now entirely out-of-date, against pierced ears (long a feature of trashy girls).

ii

In this essay I am interested in overlapping types of generations: family, cultural, historical, and literary, as marked notably by modern wars. What, beyond dates and bare biological facts, constitutes generational identity? This inquiry can be taken objectively but also subjectively, existentially—a search for something like Søren Kierkegaard's "truth," "an objective uncertainty" that the individual nevertheless holds fast.

Webster's defines *generation* (from the Latin *generatus*, connected to *genus*) thus: "1. (a) a body of living beings constituting a single step in the line of descent from an ancestor; (b) a group of individuals born and living contemporaneously; (c) a group of individuals having contemporaneously a status"—such as in a school; "(d) a type or class of objects developed from an earlier type"; and "2. the average span of time between the birth of parents and that of their offspring"—the chief chronological use of the word. (A few additional meanings are given.) In the Old Testament, the term, used in the first sense (with several nuances), indicates by extension waves of people in the past and waves to come—the seed of Abraham, numberless as the stars. Phrases such as "for perpetual generations" (Genesis 9:12), "unto all generations" (Exodus 3:15), and "to a thousand generations" (Deuteronomy 7:9) are among scores of similar expressions, which extend into the New Testament, where Saint Matthew begins his Gospel with the "generation" (meaning in this instance *ancestry*) of Jesus Christ and gives the number of generations (14 in each case) between Abraham and David, David and the Babylonian exile, and the Babylonian exile and Christ. The phrase also involves, explicitly, the Hebrews' covenant with God, as in the Deuteronomy passage, which is a reference to the Lord's faithfulness. This historical and ethnic application of the word stresses the endurance of a people and its God in a prolonged vision of the future. It is not particular but general, even eschatological.

For others, the word *generations* similarly indicates *continuity*, that of the all-important genetic inheritance (the concern for which we share with animals, despite our individuality) and of social groups: family, tribe, nation (from *natio*: birth, race). This is a protectionist position; one perpetuates one's own genes and those of the group, which may be understood narrowly. As late as 1909, as Maurice Barrès illustrated in his novel *Colette Baudoche*, the French could view the Germans across the Rhine as being of different blood. Similarly, Cecil Rhodes considered the Dutch and English to be two "races." This closed-community conservatism lasted in France for decades after Barrès. The stability, cohesion, and conservatism of French society generally (except in Paris, the crucible of unrest, and certain industrialized areas)—all discernible until increased prosperity and new means of communication and travel changed the social landscape totally (around 1960)—have been attributed to the arrangement by which parents worked in the fields or in small shops or cottage industries while grandparents minded the children.

The enthusiasm for genealogy in America now is proof enough that past generations still count for present ones in vital ways. It is not historical curiosity, but rather a desire to know oneself existentially through predecessors. Reflections on oneself and one's forebears and descendants, often as a family tree (a lovely organic metaphor), lead people to consult genealogical websites and travel to ancestors' towns to search, on gravestones and in official and informal documents, for names, records of immigration, baptismal, marriage, and death dates, and other vital facts.

iii

Any generation can be described by what is known of its distinctive products and customs—diet, housing, industry, fashions, arts, institutions. For evidence of subjective, lived experience, one turns to art, literature, cinema, history (as a human science), biography, and philosophy. Painting may depict objective features (often so easily identifiable that, as Marcel Proust observed, all the portraits of figures from Louis XIV's reign, for instance, look alike); but it does not offer easily the sense of elapsed time and generational relationships, though certain 18th- and 19th-century canvases suggest them: portraits of artists' mothers and fathers (Jean-Baptiste Camille Corot, James Whistler), scenes showing a nursing mother (Jean-François Millet) or children (Berthe Morisot, Gwen John), burial scenes (Gustave Courbet), the remnants of a defeated generation (Horace Vernet's "Waterloo Soldier"). Literature, in contrast, is a treasure of examples—think of the number of works dealing with fathers and sons—and can be a generational phenomenon itself—for instance, the Generation of '98 in Spain and post-World War II authors in Germany. I shall look later at this matter, chiefly in France. First, however, a digression into the obvious. Even as I assume subjective understandings of *generation*, I must acknowledge that generations are known and experienced by their material conditions, including the products and customs just alluded to. That does not signify determinism; while material conditions shape surroundings, define certain possibilities, and impose their order, they do not *dictate* character, which is always *beyond* or *trans*-circumstances and situation. Material conditions are felt, interpreted, not simply endured.

Take travel and communication. In 1843, Victor Hugo (born 1802) was on a holiday visit with his mistress to the Atlantic coast. In newspapers they picked up in Rochefort-sur-Mer, he read, to his horror, that his newly married daughter Léopoldine had drowned five days before, in a boating accident on the Seine. Even with money at his disposal and a sense of urgency that he tried to impart to coachmen, the journey to Paris (350 miles) took him 74 hours, including the last lap, by railroad (the coach having been loaded onto a car). Léopoldine had been buried by the time he arrived. Was his grief greater than that of a father who learns, say, by telephone that his daughter has been killed and rushes to the scene? No; but he could not respond as a man would now, and the hours of agony in the coach allowed him to live over and over in his mind the terrible event with an increasing sense of frustration. Additionally, although he might have rationalized the love affair, which was not a recent one, by the fact that his wife had taken a lover earlier, a strong conviction of guilt and consequent self-reproach assailed him.

Other techniques and scientific advances shape our understanding of *generation*: People speak of the last generation to get polio, the thalidomide generation, the one that saw Sputnik or watched man walk on the moon. Rapid developments of recent years have accelerated turnover. Thus the term *generation* means increasingly "a type or class of objects usually developed from an earlier type" and "a group of individuals having contemporaneously a status" (by virtue of their exposure to these objects). One hears "those who grew up with VCRs," "the computer generation," "the DVD generation," "YouTube children," and so on. Continuity is no longer assumed or, apparently, desired; discontinuity, the new, is the rule. It is a truism that children now instruct parents and grandparents in the use of technical devices and procedures.

Wars and their aftermath, with revolutions, strikes, coups, and changes of regime (so many in France!), have likewise served as generational watersheds. When I asked an acquaintance what the word *generations* suggested to her, she replied immediately, "Veterans"; she worked at the VA hospital for decades and saw the wounded of five or six wars. In France, those who fought in the squares with Napoleon or lived through the retreat from Russia, those who fought in the first colonial campaigns (starting in 1830), those who were beaten by the Prussians or participated in the violent fighting of the Commune saw themselves in each case as a generation by virtue of these experiences. In America, the 1861-65 war similarly defined a generation. The two world wars, the French wars in Indochina and Algeria, the American wars in Korea and Vietnam, and other 20th-century and early 21st-century conflicts similarly provided generational markers for combatants and noncombatants alike.

Generations are also identified by decades (the 60's Generation and '68 in France) or presidential administrations, especially those of Roosevelt and (often pejoratively) Eisenhower. Two well-known labels come from demographic facts, the Baby Boom and the Baby Bust. Geography, economic conditions, opportunities can furnish identity: the first generation of the New South, the GI Bill generation, the Civil Rights generation, when the overturn of Jim Crow laws and adoption of additional civil-rights codes acted as generational markers—one rode the bus or went to school "before" or "after" Rosa Parks and James Meredith. Then there are literary, art, and music monikers. Countless youths identified with the Beat Generation; others speak of themselves as belonging to the Big Band generation, or to Rock 'n' Roll. Why not dances, too—the generation of the waltz, the foxtrot, the twist, disco. As popular culture has come to dominate high culture, its characteristics have bled onto the cultural landscape and created hallmarks. The phenomenon of Woodstock (1968) brought together several strands of pop culture—music, drugs, free love, political protest—to create a "Woodstock generation."

In addition, one must mention defining generational waves of immigration into America, notably around 1900 and after 1945, then after 1970. In postcolonial and multicultural England and France such waves have exercised enormous influence, dividing many phenomena into "before" and "after." Whole neighborhoods in major cities—Paris, Los Angeles, London—have been so changed that those whose grandparents or parents lived there have become the generation that cannot go home. Foreign languages have acquired new status as co-languages in schools and elsewhere with the native tongue.

Recent generations have odd names, detached from historical boundaries. "Generation X" for post-Boomers (a term credited to Charles Hamblett) has little descriptive value beyond its algebraic use as "unknown." Next came Generation Y or 13, or the dreadful solipsistic "Me Generation," almost oxymoronic, since the "Me" types, specialists in self-promotion, tend to avoid procreation; they have been "generated" and, as one writer put it, developed "by the business of so-called art," but may abort their own progeny or simply avoid having any. They seem to feel themselves immortal (like Ernest Hemingway's Nick Adams). Atomistic in their approach and yet herd-like, throwing themselves over cultural cliffs, they may end up without a sense of identification.

iv

"**Bliss was it in that dawn to be alive,**" wrote William Wordsworth of the French Revolution, despite the destruction wrought by the Terror. As Robert Gildea shows in his *Children of the Revolution* (2008), the whole of French history from 1800 to 1914 can be viewed generationally, starting with the Romantics. François-René de Chateaubriand, strictly a pre-Romantic, born (1768) under the Old Regime, went into exile under the Revolution, then depicted the first great loner and whiner of the new century in his novella *René* (1805) and inspired a new mode of feeling—the *mal de René*, or *mal du siècle*, composed of melancholy, cultivation of solitude, the fetishization of nature, taste for the Middle Ages, and religious sentimentality. The model was widely imitated. Victor Hugo is said to have proclaimed in 1816, "I want to be Chateaubriand or nothing!" In 1820, the first major poetic collection of the movement in France, *Méditations*, by Alphonse de Lamartine, similarly drew on personal feeling and identification with nature—what John Ruskin would call the pathetic fallacy. A more vigorous, if histrionic, Romanticism came on the scene in the 1820's, with Stendhal's manifesto *Racine et Shakespeare*, novels and plays by Charles Nodier, Victor Hugo, and Alexander Dumas *père*, Hugo's poems, and other self-conscious innovations. Still later, a generation of younger writers developed *le bas romantisme*, which did not endure much past mid-century.

Some Romantic authors of great talent felt themselves out of place. Though Stendhal (born 1783) participated in Napoleon's campaigns, including the retreat from Russia, his hero Julien Sorel (in *The Red and the Black*) can only read the bulletins from the Grande Armée; in 1830, nostalgia alone remains. Stendhal felt misplaced chronologically as an artist: He believed (correctly) that his writing would not truly be appreciated until 1880 or so. The officer-poet Alfred de Vigny (born 1797) likewise complained that he and his contemporaries had arrived too late; service in peacetime was servitude, not glory. (His imagination had been stirred by tales of military exploits from the mid-18th century told by his father, aged 60 when Vigny was born.) His pessimism may have sprung from this disappointment. He also felt ill at ease with industrialization. (See, on railroads, his poem "The Shepherd's Hut.") The poet Alfred de Musset (born 1810) saw himself (through his hero

Rolla) as in a time "out of joint." "I have come too late, into a world too old." Musset's poetry, though lyrical, is tinged with irony, an un-Romantic attitude.

Another outstanding French literary generation is that of the early 1900's, the Belle Epoque but also the prologue to vast destruction and upheaval. A first wave consisted of major figures (Paul Claudel, Paul Valéry, Charles Péguy, Gide, Proust) born around 1870; it was followed by a second wave of very talented authors born in the 1880's. All of them witnessed the Great War; some were killed (Péguy, Alain-Fournier). A later wave was composed of writers born in the 1890's, old enough (or just barely) to see action. In addition to being marked by the Dreyfus Affair, many Frenchmen of that decade felt singled out by fate, responsible for retrieving the territory lost after the Franco-Prussian War. Passage of the law requiring three-year military service and two diplomatic crises—Tangiers in 1905 and Agadir in 1911—foreshadowed the coming conflict, in which the *classes* (a military term) that were called up year after year were like *generations* in a school. Numbers of mediocre novels were written about the Lost Provinces and the need for national sacrifice.

Proust's masterpiece illustrates the ruptures brought by war. In the early parts of *Remembrance of Things Past*, society appears stable; classes are well defined, and only a few upper bourgeois penetrate the aristocracy. Pressures on stability are reflected, however, arising from the Dreyfus Affair and diplomatic confrontations. Then, in wartime, social distinctions are blurred, barriers eliminated, and society seems turned on its head. Accompanying this change is the death of some, including the narrator's great friend Saint-Loup, and the dramatic, if inevitable, aging of survivors, who seem like ghosts of themselves.

The Great War meant the decimation of a generation, culturally as well as demographically. Poetry and fiction were affected through the interwar period, which Robert Graves and Allan Hodge called *The Long Weekend*. The term "Lost Generation," applied to American writers abroad after 1918, fits even better Europeans and others whose lives were so disrupted, or whose minds or bodies were so affected, that they could not function well. Jake in Hemingway's *The Sun Also Rises* and Daniel—a philanderer who loses his manhood—in Martin du Gard's *Les Thibault* are emblematic of the larger problem. The Great Depression created a new generation of committed, or engaged, writers, communist-leaning often—not Hemingway, Faulkner, nor François Mauriac in France, but many others.

I am of this interwar period. "Depression child," I say of myself; war child also. My father was not without work in the 1930's; after his grocery business failed, he returned to teaching, for which he was well qualified by character and intellect, but his salary was very low. Nevertheless, my parents helped out a family named Shields, who came to visit on occasion. Other features of the time remain in memory: ragpickers in the alley, hoboes my grandmother fed at her back door, door-to-door salesmen selling needles, bread and soup lines. Circumstances shaped demography. Many of my contemporaries and I were only children; few families of my acquaintance had more than two or three. My husband's father, who had won the County Dublin singing contest at age 16, immigrated around 1910 and later gained his American citizenship by enlisting in the Army in 1917. Gassed, he came home with badly damaged lungs, developed tuberculosis, and died in the 1930's, leaving a widow with a very small pension and three children. My husband started his studies at a state university but could not afford to return after the first year; only an NROTC scholarship at Rice allowed him to continue. My father's brother Jack, one of what Tom Brokaw called "the greatest generation," practiced civil law in the 1930's but had few clients and often managed to reconcile them before cases were heard. As a result, he could not make a living. Hence, he joined the Navy, and died from burns in the Battle of Leyte Gulf in 1944. Three cousins (Beth Bradshaw among them) and another uncle were likewise in the Armed Forces. At home, protein and fat foods, sugar, coffee, shoes, gasoline were rationed and scarce; medical care was not easily obtained either. These are, if you will, minor deprivations and discomforts compared to the death, often torture, of millions. Indeed. But they were decisive for me and many of my age. So I rejoin Great-Aunt Margaret, whose girlhood was likewise marked by war.

V

Aunt Flora, the next-to-last of her generation to go, has been dead now for 30 years. My late cousins Jean and Edith, and I also, resembled her increasingly as we aged (like the narrator's mother, in Proust's novel, who grows into her own mother, as it were). Jean looks much like her; Edith used to say my speech resembled hers; we all laughed like her. My daughter will remember her for decades to come. Today I opened, on the piano, a songbook that bears an inscription in my grandfather's elegant handwriting: "To my daughter Flora, 1948." In her honor, I played Scottish and Irish songs: "The Blue Bells of Scotland," "Loch Lomond," "Skye Boat Song," and "Bendemeer's Stream." Every day, I think of her and my wonderful parents and grandparents. At least I know my biological origins; it is distressing that some people do not. The ancient questions remain for all, however; Gauguin asked, it will be recalled: "Where do we come from? Who are we? Where are we going?"

Literature and Its Contents

At night, when lamplight turns curtain-framed windows into small proscenium stages, I like to look into houses, and lives, whether through the high, spacious panes that open into drawing rooms along St. Charles Avenue in New Orleans, or the narrow windows of shotgun houses on the side streets. This is not voyeurism. There is a tendency now amongst some pretentious critics to connect all visual enterprises, beyond utilitarian activities dependent upon the eye, with the unsavory impulse to spy on others, perhaps to patronize them, to possess them, to undergo their sensations without cost: their danger and desire, the spectator's thrill. This would be oppression, so widespread as easily to go unrecognized—the sort of unconscious exploitation that certain social critics rejoice to identify. If one takes strictly this view (dare I use the word?), all painting is voyeuristic, all theater and cinema—indeed, why not all biography, history, and literature, where we "see" mentally and experience life without consequences; why not, ultimately, all sympathetic movements toward others? But if these are voyeurism, another word will have to be found for the perversion to which specialists apply the term.

So: I like to catch glimpses of people's houses and, better, to be invited there; perhaps, like Honoré de Balzac, I believe that their place and mode of living reveal their character. Depending on what can be found, I also like to look into their minds—not to pry, not to "explain," but to be enlightened by their reflections, entertained by their wit, perhaps moved by the personal dramas taking place on this inner stage, so narrow in the cranium, so vast in scope. Best of all is to look into the great minds of the past who have expressed themselves in autobiography, history, philosophy, painting, and especially literature.

My opening theater metaphor was not chosen at random: for the encounter between individuals and reality has been expressed and explored better in drama and other literary genres than in almost any other medium or area of human endeavor (philosophy being their chief rival, I suppose). Thus I want to consider in these pages literature and its contents. (The accent is on the second syllable, not the first. Oh, these English homographs! But of course the contentment comes from the contents, as from the form, and their ineffable blend.) In the course of these reflections, something will come out of my own preferences and enduring concerns, as they underlay my professional career and endure on the far side of it. Through the sort of exchanges that can be called "readerly intertextuality" (the term is explained just below), good literature furnishes communication with others and extension of the mind. If Michel Butor, a contemporary novelist and critic, could say that he wrote "in order to become more intelligent," surely we all *read* to do so. Were we not told that reading maketh a full man? Or so I should hope. I should hope, likewise, that it would be a tasty as well as nourishing meal.

In "Tradition and the Individual Talent," T.S. Eliot argued that the literature of the past was the necessary foundation and context for that of the present. With different terminology and a different emphasis, Mikhail Bakhtin proposed, in critical work composed at roughly the same time but translated only later into Western European languages, what he called *dialogism* in literature and culture—the plurality of voices within and among texts, the interweaving of cultural threads. In the late 1960's, at the hands of his Bulgarian follower Julia Kristeva, the principle of dialogism was modified to produce the notion of intertextuality—strictly speaking, the presence of a text in another, through quotation, allusion, borrowed rhetorical patterns, and so forth; more broadly, any interpenetration of works by others, or the functioning of a text as a response to other voices. Whether coming from the archconservative Eliot, or critics whose cultural views were formed under state socialism, these positions assume alike the cultural contexts of a literary work, and, by extension, the making of a mind through others. If "each man's mind is his very self," to quote Samuel Pepys's motto, it nevertheless depends on cultural products, which afford, beyond basic cognitive tools, vast resources in many domains through which the mind becomes developed and in turn develops its own products; and literature is not the least of these resources.

The status of literature and of its tradition now must be, however, a matter of grave concern. The loss of literacy and the declining acquaintance with the great writers of the past (and present) have been discussed at length by numerous American critics, including E.D. Hirsch, Jr., Harold Bloom, John Ellis, and Norman Fruman, who all have suggested some approaches toward remedying the matter, although Bloom nearly despairs of a solution. The matter has both an economic and a cultural side. The literary publishing houses of New York have been swallowed into conglomerate enterprises that are interested chiefly in books that will sell 500,000 copies in the chain bookstores. Good editors have practically disappeared, to judge by publishers' products, and literary journals are greatly reduced in number. Solid acquaintance with foreign languages has diminished; this hits me where it hurts—for instance, the French-language bookstores I used to patronize in New Orleans have closed. Reading at the college level, and among many post-college adults, has become a sort of fast-food experience; students consume fewer things of quality, and their understanding and ability to read have diminished correspondingly.

In particular, with the challenges to the canon of major works, because of prejudice against what is seen as an elite aestheticism and on other political grounds, a different understanding of *what* and *how* to read has come to prevail. Anatole France defined literary criticism as "the adventures of a soul among masterpieces." But the notion of "masterpiece" has been assailed dreadfully; as for the soul, it has been out of fashion for ages now. The method to be applied to any canonic piece is deconstruction—determining its alleged linguistic, social, and political masquerading, reducing it to self-exposé and self-annihilation, or a web of nonreferentiality. (One of the results of the decline in reading is that students have lost the ability to handle systems and patterns and expect nothing less than ease in their studies, and in life. Their intelligence exercises itself on only the least resistant paths, scarcely apt to deal with the new, the demanding, the changing—whereas one of the great utilities of a liberal-arts education, as Jacques Barzun wrote in *Academic Questions* and as I assert later in this volume, is that it develops the mind so that it can handle a range of challenges, including incorporating the unknown into the known, utilizing new methodologies, and rejecting the flawed. To make the point to my readers, doubtless, is to preach to the converted. Except in Hyde Park, they are preachers' usual audience; occasionally, I suppose, those who remain to pray had come to scoff.)

The declining status of literature, and its consequences, are particularly noticeable in the area to which I have devoted much of my life, the study of French literature. I should say something about how I came to it. Thanks to well-read and constantly quoting parents, I grew up on Shakespeare and various other English-language poets and prose writers—among them John Milton, Alexander Pope, Jane Austen, Wordsworth, Alfred Lord Tennyson, William Butler Yeats, and quotable 19th-century American poets—and of course I read early on, in translation, bits of Voltaire, Victor Hugo, and Guy de Maupassant. At the feet of a severe Texas schoolmaster named Mr. Slover, whose eyes, behind heavy spectacles, I can still see casting rapidly about the classroom for evidence of student obstinacy or, less often, understanding, I learned something of the Spanish literary tradition. Finally, discovering French at age 17 and French literature in the text not long after, I was smitten, and remain so to this day, holding the best-written products of that tongue to be both an end in themselves, for their wit, music, and verbal brilliance, and a means toward understanding other things. At the time, the high regard in which such writings were held generally, based not on snobbery but on their demonstrable excellence, supported me. As I asserted in the foreword to *French Culture 1900-1975*, France has occupied a preeminent position in learning and the fine arts during most periods starting with the High Middle Ages. Around 1900 it dominated Western culture to an unprecedented degree, and continued to do so during much of the past century. The notion of taste was more developed and more honored there than anywhere else, and, traditionally, the loftiest, most refined cultural products have occupied an important place in the collective life and education, starting in grammar school. It is in this role as high culture that French literature was long respected on American campuses, along with the language, a solid knowledge of which was one of the badges of education.

But, as the challenge to masterpieces indicates, high culture has been under particular attack; the word *canonic* is not a compliment. (Thus in an article on "The New Formalism" *The Raintown Review* "critic" Quincy Lehr attacked the present author for what he considered "prissy preciousness" in echoes of the literary canon.) The refined has lost its status, and in some circles it would seem almost as odd to boast of one's acquaintance with it as to wear a lavalliere tie. In the United States it does remain protected in selected museums, symphony orchestras, a few art cinemas, some monthlies and quarterlies, and a very limited number of other cultural manifestations—a kind of cultural zoo for threatened species—outnumbered and offset by bad ephemeral art, pop orchestras, watered-down intellectual magazines, and, of course, the vast quantities of mass-media products and other popular phenomena. On campuses, high culture is similarly assailed, and those in departments of English, foreign literatures, ancient and European history, music, and art history have all felt blowing down their collars the two-headed dragon's breath of the "practical" and "relevant," on one side, and the "correct" (that is, multicultural, feminist, and so on) on the other.

French departments are not the least vulnerable to curricular and budgetary pressures, which can be exercised because the students no longer value, or suppose others will value, the recondite matters that constitute upper-level course work. The French language they may still want to study; but, as the steamer trunks and sturdy suitcases of yesteryear have been replaced by backpacks and soft nylon or tapestry bags for stowing necessarily rumpled traveling clothes in overhead bins of planes, the reading of Blaise Pascal, Jean Racine, Balzac, Lamartine, Claudel, Proust—which, we once thought, qualified one as educated, ready to move on to the rest in life—has yielded to more utilitarian enterprises. The students want skills that will help them beat out the competition in the practical world: business French, conversation, or a condensed soup of vocabulary and useful information to facilitate their work or travel in a Francophone area. Alas, I cannot teach business French, nor desire to. If I had wanted to go into international finance or management, would I not have done so years ago? As for what colleagues want, it is illustrated in the established track in so-called literary theory, and some have recently taken to instituting courses along the lines of "French Feminisms" and "The Body in Nineteenth-Century France"—a fancy title for the study of prostitution.

Department chairmen, course organizers, and textbook companies have, you may be sure, sought to oblige the students to the fullest, in the name of utility and with an eye on the bottom line. One cannot get a good grammar textbook these days, and anthologies of French literature of the standard repertory are virtually all out of print, but one has a wide choice of practical texts and those consisting of cultural mush *cum* random bits of language. The tendencies of the day are well illustrated in a textbook (chosen by a former colleague) used in a multisection course. There are very few selections from the great names of French literature, too canonic; exceptions are made for Colette, doubtless because she is a woman, and, remarkably, for three standard 19th-century writers. The text is inadequate in other ways also, including editorial obtuseness about what requires glossing and ignorance of certain lexical niceties, but has the requisite multicultural element, thanks to a selection of texts from Canada, the Antilles, and Africa. It also contains a section dealing with graphic and verbal advertisements for beer and the like—they too are seen as "texts," full of semiological meanings. Particularly telling—and condescending toward both its audience and its contents—is the book's stated aim, namely, to persuade students that literature can be a prime-time activity. (No need for me to put quotation marks around this last expression; it is plain from my title that I would not take such a reductionist attitude—for that is what it is, comparing literature to the coarse, intrusive, and debased fare of the opiate hour.)

There is a serious misunderstanding, however, in the quasi-rejection, on "liberal" grounds, of the traditional great writers—as the evolution of French literature itself illustrates. Far from being a garotte that would strangle the emergence of any forms beyond accepted boundaries, or exclude radical thought, taste and tradition in France have served also, almost from the beginning, to elicit their antithesis: the bold and adventurous in contrast to the routine; the coarse in contrast to the refined; the overflowing in contrast to the restricted; the freethinking in contrast to the pious. Contradicting, correcting, mocking, even subverting seem to be basic, and healthy, human needs. In particular, our desire to revere and stylize both life and death, manifested in ritual and myth among all cultures with which I am familiar and doubtless many more, is counterbalanced by our need to subvert this reverence, to see life as a comedy, now hilarious, now gruesome, played out by a basically unaesthetic and vulgar body and a mind given to all sorts of posturing. Likewise, the need for order is tolerable only when violations of this order are possible, made so by and within the very order itself. As Pierre Albert-Birot wrote in a manifesto of 1916:

> The French Tradition: is to break the shackles
> The French Tradition: is to see and understand everything
> The French Tradition: is to search, discover, create . . .
> Therefore the French Tradition IS TO NEGATE THE TRADITION
> Let's follow the tradition . . .

Gide, who was himself, in his term, a creature of dialogue, wrote, without apparently having heard of the Russian critic Bakhtin and his now-famous notion of dialogism, that French literature was a great exchange of voices that counterbalanced one another. This is true in both aesthetic form and thought; when sclerosis of form sets in, new modes break through, while certain tendencies nevertheless are maintained from century to century. *The Romance of the Rose*, as first worked out by Guillaume de Lorris in the 13th century as a refined, courtly allegory, elicited its counterpart, so to speak, in the continuation by Jean de Meung, in which refinement gives way to crude realism, satire, and social criticism. The same courtly tradition and subversion of it, as well as various other late-medieval strains of writing, when added to the new humanism, contributed in the 16th century to the monumental cornucopia of François Rabelais, who, as Bakhtin saw, is a subversive writer, and yet a major figure of the canon. (If, for eroticism and pornography—a term from the Greek, devised in France in the 18th century—the Marquis de Sade and his latter-day follower Georges Bataille stand out, you can't beat Rabelais for sheer coarseness.) Then there is Etienne Dolet, one of my favorites among the French Renaissance humanists, a rebellious, iconoclastic polymath, biblical scholar, and editor of Rabelais, who paid for his opinions and contributions to learning by being imprisoned repeatedly and hanged in 1546.

In the early 17th century, the Huguenot and freethinking poet Théophile de Viau, who urged that everyone write in his own style instead of imitating models, was imprisoned, then banished, for having taken part in assembling the *Satirical Parnassus*, a licentious work. The appearance of Pascal in roughly the same period was a counterweight not only to Michel de Montaigne and his skepticism but to this vein of libertinism (intellectual as well as moral), which was later taken up by some of the Enlightenment writers—Denis Diderot, Voltaire, and others—who posed further threats, too, to institutions and beliefs; yet they also are of the canon. Even Proust was subversive; after all, he was accused, early on, of not knowing how to write and undermining the form of the novel. One would not be far off the mark in concluding that French literature has *everything*, weights and counterweights, aesthetic refinement of the highest level and an offsetting coarseness, orthodoxy and heterodoxy, order and disorder, the principle of "nothing to excess" (as Gide wrote, "French classicism tends entirely toward litotes") and the principle of literary surfeit, and that what is meant by "canonic" includes both the radical and idiosyncratic, on the one hand, and the central and traditional, on the other.

I have spoken so far largely in general terms. Clearly, there is also at stake in these reflections something personal—if you wish, existential. Is its continual self-contestation and dialoguing what makes French literature hold me so? An English-language writer, I nevertheless have spent much of my life with French prose and verse. That itself creates a double linguistic life in my head. Within the French, I listen to a choir of voices in a polyphonous exchange, which affords both the validation and the counterpart of my neuroses and idiosyncrasies. Johann Wolfgang von Goethe said, "I call the healthy genre *classical*, and *romantic* the literature of sickness"; Gide added, "Classicism is tamed romanticism." I need both. A restless, compulsive poet and essayist with a mania for order as well as attraction to disorder, loving rationality but, even more, the harmonics of feeling and word that go beyond the rational, drawn toward anticlericalism as toward genuine religious conviction, appreciating the duke of La Rochefoucauld's one-line aphorisms and a short lyric by Guillaume Apollinaire as much as the vast fictional worlds of Balzac and Proust, knowing the appeal of the raw and untamed, as of the most refined (the wilds of the American West *versus* Paris, if you will), I managed to teach at the same institution for nearly 30 years and find happiness in routine only through vicarious experience and a developed imaginative life, including the consumption and sometimes production of the written word. Pascal spoke of *divertissement*—the diversions to which we cling; Charles Baudelaire entitled one of his prose poems "*Chacun sa chimère*"—a private monster for each of us. All are cripples in a sense, clutching onto beliefs, ideas, purposes, any screen in front of the abyss. (On the matter of slavery to language, I cannot do better than quote from W.H. Auden's "In Memory of W.B. Yeats." Time, he writes, though intolerant to youth and beauty,

> Worships language and forgives
> Everyone by whom it lives;

Pardons cowardice, conceit,
Lays its honors at their feet.

Thus, he adds, Kipling found pardon, and Claudel, pardoned for "writing well." Auden was right to speak of pardon for Claudel: an impossible man, intolerant, bombastic, willfully closed-minded, bullying, but at his best a splendid poet.)

I have enjoyed an evening, or a semester, with the witty criticism and exquisite regular verses of the very Cartesian Valéry, where nothing is to excess and where, from the raw data of perception and thought, verbal beauty and "music" create in the mind art objects both sensual and rational; and I can take pleasure in Jean de Meung's satire on the clergy or laugh at an episode of the *Roman de Renart* in which the fox rapes the wife of his rival and uncle, Ysengrin the Wolf, as she is caught in a doorway. (It turns out that she likes it, and tells him so. However, when, encouraged by her pleasure, he again performs the deed some days later, she protests and cries *rape*. Thus we have an early literary instance of "acquaintance rape" and charges brought after the fact, owing to caprice.)

Literature affords me also, however, contact with deep and moving layers of experience. It is where the most ordinary joins the finest, which lays claim to our attention as finest when it deals supremely well with what is most fundamental and meaningful to all. In 1930 the French publisher Bernard Grasset, a conservative, wrote, using italics, that "a certain degree of knowledge of humankind, and of its welfare, cannot be surpassed, and that *this degree was reached from the first ages when man began to think*." While the unfortunate uses to which such a dogma could be put, in the Europe of the 1930's, do not escape us now, there is insight in his statement: Certain elements of the human condition are known to nearly all, and have been known for tens of millennia, as primitive graphic art, artifacts, and burial customs suggest. I recall reading of an ancient lamentation, transmitted through oral tradition and quoted by anthropologists working in Tierra del Fuego: A mother mourned the death of her child, aged two, complaining that "he was too young to die." And so mothers have grieved throughout time, as, in a different mode, the composer Herbert Howells grieved upon the death of his young son, for whom he wrote a *Requiem* in 1936 as his own lamentation. Mme. de Sévigné, a member of the landed aristocracy under Louis XIV, close to the royal court, displayed in her letters to her daughter, separated from her by many leagues and a new marriage, the same solicitude and anxieties that parents showed long before and long after for their absent offspring; social privilege did not remove her from the common human condition. The difference between her and others was that she expressed her concerns in such a way that, 300 years later, I read them as though they were mine—and even my students have acknowledged that their parents display similar concerns. One need have no learning to experience the basic needs of the body and the heart, the mystery of sexual union and birth, the wonder of growth, the pain of failure and error, the dread of suffering and death, the claims of the social order, and the indifference and resistance of the natural world; but the reflective and formal expression of these basic ingredients of human experience in art and literature gives them another dimension—redeems them to some degree, if you will. The French say, by the verb *approfondir*, that it *deepens* them. The finest art of Shakespeare, in its supreme moments in *Hamlet* and *King Lear*, deals with these very matters, which are transcultural. "Pray you, undo this button."

Perhaps one of the best illustrations in French of what a single writer can afford is Proust—although many others could serve as examples. I was introduced to Proust in full at age 21 by a brilliant exophthalmic professor, himself somewhat Proustian, who later left the university abruptly in midterm, the scandals of his private life having seeped through and come to officials' attention. I have sometimes told students, in jest, that acquaintance with Proust is useful because it helps them understand *New Yorker* cartoons. These are scarcely grounds, however, on which to justify the reading of 3,000-plus pages (small print in the Pléiade edition). Known (rightly) as a social and cultural snob, who spent much of his time flattering people and insinuating himself into fashionable salons and later devoted hundreds of pages to descriptions of dinners and receptions, and also known (again, justly, though less than people believe) for a difficult, challenging style, which piles clause upon clause, uses adjectives in abundance (up to seven for one noun, yet never too many), accumulates parenthetical phrases, and teases the mind by postponing the main verb, Proust is certainly a supreme example of elitist culture, perhaps the most strikingly so in France since Racine perfected classical tragedy in rhymed alexandrines at the time of the Sun King. Yet I have profited enormously from reading the whole of *Remembrance of Things Past* five times, some parts many more, and once or twice everything else Proust wrote except some letters; so that, when a student once expressed great surprise that I had not seen a certain movie starring Julia Roberts (whose name I barely knew), I could counter that at least I had read Proust (whose name he knew even less) five times. What is in this for anyone, besides a tart answer to an ingenuous undergraduate? Here is what I would tell the skeptical, pointing out that one need not read all seven parts of the vast novel to enjoy these riches, and thus hoping through this menu to draw new readers to Proust's banquet, or cocktail buffet.

Stendhal defined the novel as "a mirror carried along a road," reflecting and showing us how to see the dramas of life. Proust's masterpiece reveals, by means of the segment of society that interested the novelist, how the world works—the mechanisms of ambition, desire, rivalry, and power, the value of exclusivity, the fragility of position, the dynamics of groups. His great social portraits (Mme. Verdurin, the Duchesse de Guermantes, Swann, Charlus), unrivaled for their subtlety and depth, have universal value; the criticism that these figures are exceptions, only members of the upper classes whose behavior has no general truth, is invalid. Ambition, desire, rivalry, the thirst for power characterize the rabble as the rich; socialist societies have not proven to be immune from these drives, and you can see them by frequenting any barroom for a few evenings. In addition to my old professor, I have known a Charlus on my own campus; and who has not discovered, hidden under the urbanity of a refined society or professional woman, a petty spirit like that of the Duchess? Proust shows well how the same relationships operated in the world of a late-19th-century invalid—rich, old, and tyrannical—as at the court of Louis XIV, and how the mechanisms of snobbism are at work similarly at different levels, noting that the servant Françoise draws prestige, at her own social rank, from the position and manners of the family which employs her: She too is a snob. Experience bears this out. The guard at my bank, an affable chap without much education at all, inquired once whether I was a member of the exclusive Orléans Club, pointing out with no little pride that he used to work there and thus knew such eminent ladies (his term) as Mrs. Monteleone (of the Monteleone Hotel family)—in which respect he's done better than I.

One can find politics and history, too, in Proust: the Dreyfus Affair, the Great War, not as they are presented in standard historical accounts, but as they are observed and lived by witnesses. Despite their fictional status, Proust's figures offer the perspectives and very feel of the age: the tone of social events at times of political crisis, and how people are excluded because they are thought to hold the wrong opinion on Dreyfus or, later, to be Germanophiles; the atmosphere of Paris during wartime, under blackout, the snowy trees along the darkened streets recalling a Japanese painting, the air raids reminding the narrator of Wagner's Walkyries. One can test the waters of patriotism and prejudice around 1900 by watching and listening to Proust's characters, and learn to decode diplomatic language in the speech of M. de Norpois.

There are other great topics, too: suffering, death, pathologies of the body and mind (a nervous temperament, maternal fixation, sexual anomalies, insomnia, voyeurism—the real one; and, to judge by the popular media today, everyone is interested in pathology). The comments on art, music, and literature constitute a solid course in post-Realistic aesthetics, and Proust's fictitious artists—Elstir the painter, Vinteuil the musician, Bergotte the writer—present, through their careers, subtle views on the creation of art. If you like nature, you are well served: word-paintings of fields of poppies, hedgerows of eglantine and hawthorn, the sea under changing light, as in J.M.W. Turner paintings, streams filled with water lilies that, for their precision and beauty of image, rival those of Claude Monet. As for love, it is agreed that the anatomy of passion in Proust—desire, jealousy, finally their erosion in indifference—is equal to the portrait of passion in Shakespeare, Racine, and Stendhal; and, if you hesitate at tackling his lengthy analyses, you can get the essence of his insights on love and other topics in his brilliant condensations, collected as *The Maxims of Marcel Proust*. Finally there is style—not ornamentation, as some believe, but a way of seeing and understanding: establishing relations, drawing out conclusions, determining details and nuances, echoing feelings, conveying in words the visible world.

Literature, I said, is dialogue. Multilayered, it is even more than contact with a great voice of the past; we enter into contact also with many who have read the work with us, whether our friends with whom we discuss it, or those more removed who have based on it films or criticism, or built on it for other work of their own. As a specialist in modern literature, I have the advantage: It is a lens through which one can see the whole of the past. When I read Gide or Proust on Baudelaire, Gide on Montaigne, Mauriac on Racine, Valéry on Voltaire and Pascal (and thus, by intertextual triangulation, Voltaire's comments on Pascal), or my friend the late Jules Roy writing up his own amorous affairs in terms of *Dangerous Liaisons*, I am reading their reading and the original, anew. Sometimes I even read through my father's reading; he liked Stendhal's novels, and Gide's wittiest works—*The Counterfeiters*, *Oedipus*, and *Theseus*; and, as I have recorded elsewhere, when I gave him *Man's Fate* by André Malraux, surely one of the finest novels of the 20th century in any language, he was so taken with it that he could not put it down, and we often spoke of it afterward. As for iconoclasts, they need to be familiar with the tradition to overturn it; iconoclasm too supposes dialogue, intertextuality. What would parody be without the work parodied? How can we have *Don Quixote* without the chivalric romances of which it was both the finest and the most absurd? One needs to know the context in order to acquire, as Jean Cocteau wrote, "the tact of understanding just how far you can go too far."

If this is addiction, let us make the most of it. Literature has the capacity not only to delight and instruct, but to maintain and strengthen a common ground of understanding. Or are we to be islands, connected by only a weedy Sargasso Sea of popular culture and counterculture? I sometimes wonder whether, in the future, there will be any students left who will agree that they can become more intelligent by reading Proust's masterpiece and others, and who are willing to make the effort. Perhaps some of those I have taught in the past, who, like Keats, have seen through books "many goodly kingdoms," will send their sons and daughters for similar discoveries. Pathology and balance, anguish and serenity, the rare and the most ordinary, the decorative and the plain, refinements of taste and thought in a life which must needs be part of the common human condition: The range of literature is there at our disposal, a serendipitous version of the range of experience—as people say in New Orleans, the *lagniappe* of life.

The New Yorker Under the Glass

THE FIRST ISSUE OF *THE NEW YORKER* (February 21, 1925) showed on its cover a dandy in top hat, high collar, and morning suit gazing through his monocle at a butterfly. The drawing is reproduced yearly, with variations, and butterflies became a cover motif. Whatever tastes, affectations, or snobbery the artist, Rea Irvin, wanted to suggest, it is time now to turn the monocle on the magazine and subject it to scrutiny.

What the glass reveals is a very disappointing publication, if one judges by former standards. Though there had been modifications in the early years, as the magazine ceased to deal chiefly in humor and published more serious journalism and fiction, and though changes in editorship (from Harold Ross to William Shawn to Robert Gottlieb) inevitably introduced slightly different tones, there was no significant new departure until the magazine was redesigned by Tina Brown, its editor from 1992 until 1998. The aim was apparently to be modish, up-to-date; that meant campy, vulgar, even outrageous. Brown fired respected contributors (and some left on their own), hired new people, including the photographer Richard Avedon, who had specialized in fashion, and adopted a policy of amazing middle-class readers (*épater le bourgeois*). In the process, according to *Gawker.com*, she incurred losses of $70 million. Generally, the same editorial policies have been maintained by her successor, David Remnick, whose staff includes several of her appointees.

For decades, my late friend Evelyn Payne read everything in *The New Yorker*, every week, except the football articles; she would not read it now at all, given the assaults on good taste, or what the radical cultural critics call (approvingly) "transgression of boundaries." Taste and fashion, it might be argued, are culturally insignificant—Goth or retro clothing fads, slang, dark nail polish, bean-bag furniture. In fact, many such matters are important; choices in manners, speech, dress, music, literature, and film reveal us and form us—and affect others, including children, edifying them or perhaps leading them astray. That is, taste is an aspect of propriety and, ultimately, morality. It's not, as Fat Albert would have said, that *The New Yorker* has no taste; what it has is bad taste. True, bad taste can be just slovenliness; but when is that desirable? Frequently, violation of taste is intended to offend (and thus attract attention as daring), as in the mouths or on the bodies of rebellious children and youth and in the work of many writers and painters. The nude photographs in *The New Yorker* under the new dispensation were surely meant to create chic scandal—a pseudosophisticated nose-thumbing—and raise subscription numbers. As for the foul language in every issue, the wacky behavior, the intimate details, they are inspired, one might charitably suppose, by a realist impulse—to portray people as they really act and speak. Some people, that is. An article in the July 2012 issue by John McPhee—a very capable writer, by the way—traces the steps by which, after 1980, a verb popularly used in street language, and then, sometime later, various nouns and adjectives derived from it, were allowed into the magazine. I am not unaware of the arguments for Zolaesque realism in fiction and reporting; but is near-cinematographic imitation necessary in a magazine with 47 issues a year, intended to be of broad interest and widely circulated, displayed in offices and on coffee tables at home?

In addition, the general design of the magazine is no longer attractive. There are numerous sidebars, gaudy cartoons in large panels, and messy pages with distracting fonts and illustrations, as though it were directed to readers with attention deficit. Infantilism is not absent elsewhere, especially in short items in *The Talk of the Town*. While, unlike explicitly experimental magazines, *The New Yorker* does not excoriate previous models of literary worth, the latter seem to be of little concern. The fiction strikes me as generally mediocre, often dealing with jaundiced urbanites whose tales are tedious; sometimes it approaches soft porn. Similarly, the poetry is usually mediocre, sometimes incredibly bad; Michael Dickman's poems, for instance, illustrate the magazine's penchant for juvenile products echoing bad Surrealism. (The poems of Richard Wilbur, C.K. Williams, and a few others deserve praise, however.) Since 2004, a pop-music column, now by various hands but written until 2015 by Sasha Frere-Jones (a pseudonym), who wrote for the *Village Voice* earlier and is presently at the *Los Angeles Times*, has brought another type of vulgarity into the magazine. What drives pop music is mostly seriality, not personal taste; girls scream and swoon at performances because others do, and CDs and concert tickets sell on the basis that other consumers like them. Generally, the worse, the better. A television column by Emily Nussbaum, another addition to the rubrics, is a further sign of degraded taste. It is sometimes of an unspeakable vulgarity.

Facts are still checked in *The New Yorker*, presumably, but I have found significant errors, of the avoidable sort. Another departure from earlier standards is degraded grammar. Surely previous staff members, famous for their emphasis on high standards of language, especially Eleanor Gould, who occupied the position of grammarian at the magazine from 1945 until 1999, would recoil in horror from what one finds today. A frequent error, doubtless house style now, is the objective case after forms of *to be*. "It was him," "It's me" are the rule, no matter who has written the piece (including, doubtless, some who know better but bend or are overruled). Then there are errors in syntax. From the pen of David Denby, the movie critic, comes this misuse of *whom*: "a woman twenty years older—a stern, secretive, yet hungry partner whom the boy doesn't realize is a former concentration camp guard." Elsewhere, a *who* is omitted, as though the writer or copyeditor could not follow the sentence.

Plural subjects (often linked by *and*) sometimes have singular verbs, as in "the combined *salaries . . . was*" and "Operation Iron Triangles *rules* of engagement—which, they had said, *was* . . . " One finds *snuck* instead of *sneaked*, and, from the pen of John Lahr, the following solecism, perhaps immigrant-influenced: "only a month in New York" (for "who had been in New York for only a month"). The possessive apostrophe is often omitted. (Perhaps that is deliberate, a new style, now that the name of the great mountain overlooking Colorado Springs has been changed, officially, to Pikes Peak [*sic*].) One drives "slow," and there are infelicities in tenses. Increasingly, *bring* is used for *take*, as in "The old man brought the lost dog to the pound." Was he going to the pound anyway? Errors in quoted French are not unknown. The offices of a magazine probably have a dictionary; someone should learn how to use it. Then there are illogical or badly worded sentences. The sort of error that traffic reporters make during early morning newscasts appears: "If you go to the Cézanne room at the Musée d' Orsay . . . the array of masterpieces you'll find along the back wall were all painted at the end of his career." Ah, but if I don't go to that museum, what then about those masterpieces? In an issue from early 2012, I find *forward* for *foreword*. Now, these errors do not bother all *New Yorker* readers, presumably; many don't recognize them, while others would say, "So what?" I may be taken for a pretentious pedant. Does it make a difference how one writes? Yes. Language is both queen and servant of true culture. The adulterated language of today reflects depravity—the deliberate rejection of discrimination and erosion of standards.

In matters of behavior *The New Yorker* shows tolerance and permissiveness. Its interviewers seem to attach no blame to petty crime, the sale and use of illegal drugs, pornography and its peddlers, sadism, "drag" and transgendering, or other deviancy—these are just phenomena. Leslie Mann, a filmmaker interviewed breezily, talks casually about "smoking pot" in school and the use of marijuana among friends and in her husband's films. Space is given increasingly to interviews with activists in the movements to legalize marijuana and other psychedelic drugs. The head of one such organization was quoted in February 2016 as being concerned about managing "kids and cannabis in the house"; she added, "It's important to tell the other moms on play dates." Drugs are alluded to approvingly in reviews by Nussbaum and others.

In addition, socialist (or "progressive") convictions, like obsessive-compulsive behavior, justify helping oneself to others' things. Under the rubric *Sticky Fingers*, a short piece by one Miranda July, "Free Everything," enumerates the author's petty thefts, committed as a student at UC Santa Cruz (no surprise there, perhaps) and later in Portland, a profitable mode of life for which no shame or regret is expressed. Jenny Diski, reviewing a book on shoplifting, noted that, as a member of the counterculture and a hippie for life, she had no qualms about stealing large numbers of books from a shop in London, "corporate-owned"—that is, by "capitalistic hoods" (as though that excused theft). In fiction and articles profiling figures from the worlds of fashion and film, the magazine celebrates, even in its advertising, what I shall call "the homosexual life." It goes without saying that abortion is never questioned, nor the arguments against it mentioned except in ridicule. In a *Talk of the Town* column Jeffrey Toobin complained (in connection with the Stupak amendment) that "abortion services are being treated like a second-class form of medicine."

My comments will make me appear antediluvian to many readers (if they get this far), revealing prejudice against "lifestyles" now current. But "lifestyles" and actions are not neutral; they do make a difference in one's own situation and that of others. Styles have consequences, for individuals and society as a whole. A woman of some years, currently in Pittsburgh, not a prude nor an old conservative like me by any means, writes nevertheless of the chagrin, the disappointment, the guilt she continues to experience over the abortion she had as a young woman.

The choice of plays, movies, and television programs reviewed in the premier magazine of New York (for instance, Madonna's *Filth and Wisdom*) suggests a bias toward what is tawdry, shocking, vile, criminal. If this is almost all that stage and screen have to offer, at least the morally objectionable material could be noted as such. (Literature is full of rascals and criminals, but usually they are not treated with benign indifference: Macbeth comes to a bad end, and Madame Bovary poisons herself.) Instead, reviewers highlight atrocious behavior and quote vile language. In reviewing Michel Houellebecq's *The Map and the Territory*, James Wood, a learned man and a very able critic, seemed to take delight in the perversions and foul language the novelist had used in earlier works. Yet he acknowledged that Houellebecq wrote "atrocious prose" and created only "flimsy and diagrammatic" scenes, dialogues, and characters—that is, the formal structures of fiction. In other words, the book is not much good as fiction. Nor is Houellebecq much of a philosopher or social commentator. But he's fashionable in France. The current reviewer of poetry, Dan Chiasson, is indulgent to Americans' taste for smut. Describing *Supplication: Selected Poems of John Wieners*, he notes that the writing, like the man ("squalid"), is "unbelievably dirty" and provides examples.

The magazine is thus without prejudices, except, of course, toward standards of good taste and morality and toward traditionalists and conservatives of all stripes and other wrongheaded people. No mockery of "disadvantaged groups" would be allowed, but Texans may be ridiculed, along with any unreconstructed Southerner, and even the South in general, particularly South Carolina. California figures and phenomena, some on the loony side, fare better; it is recognized that their culture is a petri dish for new trends (that is, what infects the rest of the nation). In 1976 Saul Steinberg's "View of the World from 9th Avenue" suggested that the rest of the globe—depicted as a polyp attached to greater New York—was almost insignificant. This is not new; both Mary Austin and Willa Cather complained of Easterners' dismissive attitude toward the rest of the nation. Suspicious always of East Coast intellectualism, though she did survive there, Austin attacked explicitly the New York literary establishment for its dictatorial ways and general dismissal of anything regional as inferior. For a writer from the western states to be successful and recognized in the East, it was necessary, in the words of Ambrose Bierce, "to hammer and hammer again and again before the world will hear and heed."

The New Yorker is now entirely enfeoffed to the great powers of globalism and internationalism. In leafing through issues, saved more or less randomly, from the past few years, I find few expressions of American patriotism or regionalist loyalty (except, of course, loyalty to New York City, which in some ways is barely American). To judge by the contributors' names, the magazine pretends to cosmopolitan openness; such multiculturalism and xenophilia are displayed also in fiction, reportage, and reviews.

In 2004, for the first time ever, *The New Yorker* endorsed a presidential candidate (John Kerry). Four years later it endorsed Barack Hussein Obama. Numerous covers have had connections to the Obamas. Before the 2008 election, a satiric drawing showed the couple in the Oval Office, with a portrait of Osama bin Laden on the wall and an American flag burning in the fireplace; the candidate wears a turban and *salwar kameez*, and Michelle, with an Afro, sports camouflage trousers and an assault rifle slung on her back. The cartoon was intended as a *reductio ad absurdum* of charges that there was a connection between Obama and Islam. The drawing caused considerable comment; the editorship, evidently blind, had not imagined that Americans might take it at face value. A post-election cover celebrated the victory by highlighting in moonglow the *O* in the magazine title above a shot of the Lincoln Memorial bathed in light; the cover can be bought in poster form. Another showed Obama interviewing dogs for the position of First Pet. A later cover depicted Mrs. Obama as a fashionista. One December Obama was shown receiving Santa Claus in what looked like an oval room. The tone of *Talk of the Town* pieces concerning him was long that of slavish adulation. Others' objections to his administration's policies became, in *New Yorker* terms, "demonization" or a result of "disinformation." That somewhat later one could note a slight change in tone, with fewer encomia, simply underlines the initial foolish infatuation with Obama, his family, and his henchmen.

Indicative of the 2016 political direction (and fears) at the magazine are the 17 cartoons in the issue of April 25, all of which ridicule Donald Trump. A few have a bit of humor; others are wholly without charm. Among the latter is the drawing of a vaguely Trump-like figure dressed as Moses, and holding two golden tablets, telling "Little Yahweh" that he has his own commandments. Since the November 2016 election, the staff has continued to attack him in strident, almost crazed language and absurd caricatures.

Now, *The New Yorker* ownership (Condé Nast Publications) and editors may, obviously, do what they want, as long as revenues hold up; and, unless they fear repercussions, advertisers generally support "inclusiveness." (Surely, they will sell to anyone.) Ross, the first editor, declared that the magazine was "not edited for the old lady in Dubuque." No, but its readers were discriminating, and it was not disgusting and could be left, for instance, in a dentist's waiting room. Alas, now, the joke is on us. What was an eminent weekly, featuring notable writers (at random I mention E.B. White, James Thurber, Joseph Mitchell, William Trevor, Roger Angell—born in 1920 and still contributing of late), has become awful (though of course it is not all bad, and well-done articles still appear). Human beings spent untold millennia developing what can be called civilization and, then, high culture. Are we to discard it all, perverted creatures who destroy what is best?

The worst aspect of the whole matter is that *The New Yorker*'s claim to being the acme of culture is founded, in a way. Gutter and infantile tastes prevail among American consumers of print, electronic media, and entertainment; and the prevailing "inclusiveness" rules out few behaviors and celebrates iconoclasm. Dropping names of New York and Hollywood "celebrities" and winking at coarse, illegal, and perverted behavior, today's *New Yorker* snobs are right in fashion. Eustace Tilley (as the figure with the monocle was named) should drop his eyeglass, take off his dress clothes, mouth a few obscenities, and get cool.

In the Abbey

PICTURE YOURSELF VISITING a Norman abbey complex, partly ruined, partly restored. You have entered through the west gate or else the Porte Saint-Norbert (named for the founder of the Premonstratensian order, the original occupants). You note that the complex is predominantly Gothic in style, though the components date from different periods, chiefly the 18th century. The principal buildings are arranged in an irregular U-shape; they house dormitories and offices. Open excavations remain in the center of the courtyard. There are various other structures as well as outbuildings and a space known as The Farm. The damaged grange, or barn, is open and empty. It is huge; in medieval times the abbey had the monopoly on milling of grain for a large area. A bit farther is the abbey church, neither quite ruined nor well restored at the time of which I write. Since it is structurally unsound, it is condemned. But just a glance allows one to admire its handsome proportions and modern rose window. So, you walk around the courtyard, look into the grange; you are invited into the refectory or another building; you imagine yourself there in earlier centuries.

This is the Abbaye d'Ardenne, situated near a village called Saint-Germain-la-Blanche-Herbe, about nine kilometers from the city of Caen. The location is not to be confused with Les Ardennes (or L'Ardenne, as it is known in Belgium), the vast mountainous area through which German troops twice invaded the Lowland countries and France. In each case, the name *Ardenne* may come from a Celtic word for *forest*. At the Norman site, the cult of Arduina, a Celtic goddess of whom Tacitus speaks, may have left traces. The early occupants of the abbey were not monks, strictly speaking, but canons regular. The community dates from 1121; the oldest architectural portions are from the early decades of the 13th century. The donors, a married bourgeois couple from Caen, were merchants—a rare case, since founders were usually of the nobility. The abbey is close to Ouistreham (at the mouth of the Orne) and the famous Pegasus Bridge over the Caen canal, which British troops, having taken off from Dorset by glider, secured early on June 6, 1944. It was the first engagement with the enemy in the Normandy campaign.

In the summer of 1996, I was shown onto the grounds of the Abbaye d'Ardenne. But, unlike the visitor I have imagined, I stayed; that is, I lived there for one month. What was I doing there? Well, the place had been secularized long before, though it was still called an abbey and was reminiscent of what the medieval community and structures must have been. It had been sold in 1791, and its furnishings were dispersed. Sold again in 1799, it endured until 1830, then was partially destroyed; new buildings were erected subsequently. The whole remained in private hands. In summer 1944 the barn was seriously damaged by Allied shelling, as the invaders attempted to dislodge Germans occupying the site. The church—the choir and transepts of which had collapsed in 1230 and had never been rebuilt—was less affected by fighting, but shelling must have contributed to the collapse in 1947 of portions of the façade, rebuilt since in plainer style.

In 1994, the property was acquired by the Regional Council of Lower Normandy, which set to work on renovation. The council conceived a project, sponsored also by the Battle of Normandy Foundation, to invite American students to study there, with the cooperation of their universities. Tulane University was among the institutions approached and one of only two that accepted the invitation. Thus, in autumn 1995, three faculty members—my friend David Clinton, in political science, now professor at Baylor University; a colleague in the French department; and I—drew up a plan for a one-month summer program, in which the students would take two advanced courses, meeting five days a week. The courses were centered on World War II and French literature of that war, in translation.

During the winter and spring of 1996, I had been at the University of Sheffield as a visiting research professor, and I had remained in England. Thus to reach the abbey for the summer program, in July, all I had to do was cross the Channel (which I did by overnight ferry to Ouistreham rather than the Eurostar). David flew over from New Orleans; the third committee member did not participate, but we did have a visiting lecturer, the late Henry Mason, likewise in political science, who drove down from his summer home in The Hague. An episode from Henry's visit cannot be omitted. Whereas the weather had been quite cold at the outset, by the time Henry was to join us it had turned hot. The abbey had no air conditioning, of course, and he was displeased that his room was not cool. (Though born in Europe, he was entirely wedded to New Orleans air conditioning.) Unbeknownst to anyone else, he arose in the middle of the night, got in his car—without leaving a note—and drove as far as he needed to find an air-conditioned hotel. The next morning he did not appear, nor did he telephone; he was simply not there. David was anxious; what had happened? Eventually Henry did arrive back at the abbey, explaining rather casually that his quarters had been too hot. That was Henry.

Only five students enrolled in our program—a pity, given the fine opportunities for study and touring. Variety made up for small numbers. One, whom I'll call Kay, was in the Air Force ROTC program and thus on a scholarship. She was willing to work for an acceptable grade. But as the only woman student, she was, I believe, unhappy; she did not know how to take the older men. Another undergraduate, Ray, was not strong academically; perhaps he and his parents thought that he might raise his GPA a bit. A third, Hal (whose wedding David and I attended some years later), planned to pursue graduate work after getting his B.A. (and did so). He was the best writer of the three, who were all of conventional college age. We also had "Red," now deceased, who had served New Orleans in a public position for 17 years; he was working toward a master's degree, perhaps as a well-deserved treat to himself, and I recall with pleasure how much he appreciated the courses and the abbey experience. Finally, there was John, a professional librarian at Tulane, the oldest student of all; he got a tuition waiver for the course and thus came over, though, holding his doctorate in history, he scarcely needed any credit hours. After some days, a larger group from Texas A&M University and the professors arrived; our contacts were informal only. They held classes only four days a week. As general director of the establishment, we had "The Colonel," a retired American Army officer connected to the Battle of Normandy Foundation.

None of this is grand; surely the Lower Normandy Council had foreseen a more extensive undertaking, and The Colonel was, I believe, chagrined to have so few forces under his command. Subsequently, the abbey complex appears to have been utilized better. The barn had already been designated for future restoration as the new site for the Institut Mémoires de l'Edition—a research archive related to the history of French publishing and including authors' manuscripts and other materials. In 1998 other buildings became a cultural center, with colloquia, lectures, and so on. The abbey church is presently a library.

Now, I was greatly pleased at the notion of living amongst buildings of Gothic style in what had been a community of faith. Even a slight approximation of that ancient order, its good will, thoughtfulness, and service, appealed to me. I respond well to order; I like rules. Nowadays such an inclination is suspect, sometimes called fascist. But do we really want social and moral anarchy? While our life in the abbey was not ascetic, it was pleasantly regular, like being at Scout camp. Thus, grafting also my own habits onto the pattern and site proposed, I fit easily into the routine. In some respects it was not greatly different from a semester at Tulane except for the proximity of everything and everyone.

My quarters were in a lateral section of the U. That portion was clearly an 18th-century addition, classic rather than rococo; plain, but not severe, it reminded me of the Old Ursuline Convent in the French Quarter in New Orleans, built by military engineers early that same century. Since we were to take our meals in common, as the monks, or canons, did, my rooms, pleasing otherwise, had no kitchen and thus no kitchen table. Nor was there a desk. Where was I to write out notes, mark papers? Then there was the absence of curtains. Doubtless the monks had not concerned themselves with window shades, draperies. But I am a woman, and my large windows looked out over the courtyard. These deficiencies were soon remedied.

For the first week or so, the refectory was not ready to receive us; the cooks had not been hired. So we Tulanians all moseyed three times each day to a nearby village, where we had our meals at the sole café. Despite our small numbers, that was a windfall to the proprietors. Later we joined the Texas Aggies in the refectory, located in the former cellars of the abbey. The ancient kitchens having been destroyed, new facilities had been installed in one end of the caves. Those cellars had served well during the war; various local figures had taken refuge there under the Occupation. The Premonstratensian clerics would have approved: Though they had offered hospitality to all those from the four winds, they would have excepted enemy invaders. Jacques Vico, the son of the proprietors at the time, had concealed there arms and ammunition parachuted in for his Resistance network. One of those who had used the caves—we believe it was Vico himself or perhaps a brother—gave a talk to our group within those very cellars. Without boasting, he drew a realistic picture of what his Resistance group and others had done during the Occupation and of its practical value.

At the time, I was at work on a book concerning French war fiction, which came out three years later. I did not, however, assign reading to students on that basis—that is, in the hope that in their papers and examinations they would come up with data, critical insights, or useful summaries I could borrow, with or without attribution. The reading list was based first on what, from the suitable corpus of French fiction related to the conflict of 1939-45, was available in translation and at what price; a secondary consideration was to offer, from those available works, a range of authorial treatments and responses and thus give a fair, if limited, picture. Some works were introduced *via* long photocopied excerpts. The students may have chafed at the amount of reading. Meanwhile, David, by students' accounts an outstanding teacher, lectured on historical and diplomatic matters and similarly dealt out long reading assignments.

We had a van at our disposal, and David organized excursions. Among the sites were two invasion beaches; the Mémorial de Caen, a museum originally centered on World War II, since enlarged; the American cemetery at

Colleville-sur-Mer, overlooking Omaha Beach; and the German cemetery at La Cambe, originally a burial place for both German and American dead. (The Americans' remains were later transferred.) The visit to Caen let us appreciate how well the city, heavily shelled in 1944, had been restored, its two famous medieval abbeys rebuilt in handsome stone, the gardens abloom with flowers. At the American cemetery we placed a wreath in the name of Tulane. The German cemetery was fully as moving—all those young men, and numerous older officers (one said to be in his 70's) cut down by the scythe of death for a demented but powerful moral monster, far away.

Once at twilight, while David was away, Henry Mason and I were taken inside the church, despite its being off-limits. Our guide was the caretaker, who knew its architectural history. Though the edifice had been partly repaired, the vaulting had not yet been shored up. In my poem concerning the abbey, I called the church "blind"—partly because the lower-level Romanesque arches on each side are filled in with stones, but chiefly because the ogive openings of the upper nave had no glass, and, paradoxically, we "see" less well through open space than through windows, the eyes of the structure: I missed their illustration of the faith to which the church was dedicated. For one who loves the Gothic style, that visit at dusk to the great nave was pleasing as well as melancholic. I admired the pillar whose capital is decorated with "*la femme à la baratte*"—a woman with a churn. Medieval ecclesiastical art was marked by the quotidian and homely as well as the sacred, the latter properly a dimension of the former. On the pediment of the west portal, I noted with pleasure a chimera resembling an elephant.

Does all this sound terribly somber?—cemeteries, battlefields, deserted bunkers, ruins and half-ruins, some right next to us, *memento mori*, in addition to isolation—all of which would have appealed, doubtless, to the Romantics' taste for things medieval, architectural relics, and lonely, melancholic sites, but perhaps not suitable for a summer-course location. Add to that the memorial to certain Canadian dead, which we discovered tardily, located right at the abbey, in a side garden. The memorial is tasteful. Still, its presence might be viewed as morbid. On June 7, 1944, Panzer Grenadier-regiment 25 of the 12th SS Hitlerjungend Division (and most were doubtless *very* young) set up its headquarters in the abbey complex, after having been ordered there from south of Rouen. The officer in charge was Kurt Meyer. He installed himself in the turret of the church, a fine observation point, from which he observed the Canadian invaders, whose movements he could follow so well that his troops virtually trapped them. They suffered large losses. A score or so were taken prisoner that day and the next and taken to the abbey.

On June 8, it seems, 18 were executed in the garden. Two others apparently were shot later in the month. One body was discovered when the abbey was liberated in July; others were uncovered the following winter and spring. (Some sources give a total of 27 Canadians.) The precise circumstances of the killings were not clarified entirely, but Meyer was held responsible and put on trial in December 1945, charged with five war crimes, including execution of the abbey prisoners but also shooting of more than a score of POWs near villages where fighting had taken place. Although evidence against Meyer was somewhat contradictory and he denied ordering any executions, he was convicted of inciting his men to commit murder and, as commander, being responsible for the killings. Because one of the Canadian military authorities considered evidence against him circumstantial, the death sentence was shortly commuted to life imprisonment; he remained in prison until 1954.

To be sure, the rationale of the summer program was to become acquainted with Normandy and its past, read historical and fictional accounts of the D-Day invasion, its sequels, and other aspects of the war, and visit associated sites. Our students were supposed to appreciate the Occidental patrimony, including its religious and architectural history, and know at what cost Europe had been liberated from Nazism. It may have been too much, however.

It is perhaps unsurprising, then, that none of the undergraduates chose to participate in an excursion to Mont-Saint-Michel. How much ecclesiastical architecture and history can the young take? And how much time do they really want to spend with their professors? They may have fled to join the company of the A&M students. But the Aggies, with three-day weekends, had their own excursions. So maybe our bunch just slept. In any case, David, John, "Red," and I went off in the van for a long day and evening at the confines of Normandy and Brittany, to visit the great rock and its buildings, about which Henry Adams wrote so eloquently. I remember the omelettes (locally famous) that we ordered in a bistro among the shops at the lower levels, and our climb up the steep, winding path, then our arrival at the summit and our visit to the glorious chapel, a masterpiece of the Gothic art developed around Romanesque elements.

That day, we also visited Saint-Malo (an ambitious touring program, no?), from which, centuries before, many had set out for French Canada, whence some of their descendants moved to Louisiana in the Great Upheaval. Night had fallen when we stopped at a small inn near Granville for a bite to eat. "Red" furnished the comedy for the evening. Before the van had even been parked, he leapt out and disappeared, headed, we assumed, for the toilets. He did not reappear for many minutes, however; we had parked, gone into the restaurant, sat down, and still he was not there. Finally he joined us. When the waitress came to take his drink order, he asked for a Coca-Cola. Knowing the word for ice and knowing that in France ice is not served routinely, he added the word *glace.* The waitress, however, recognizing the American accent, thought he wanted a glass. She brought a minuscule Coke bottle and a glass. "*Glace*," he repeated, gesturing to the drinking glass. She smiled, as if to acknowledge that it was indeed a glass. "*Glace, glace*!" Finally she understood. At the end of the meal, he again disappeared in the rear. It was a long while before we saw him; he had managed to get lost in the darkness.

One evening David, the graduate students, and I enjoyed drinks and dinner at a bar-café in Autie, one of the villages where Canadians were executed. Somehow, people there learned that David was "Professor Clinton." Since William Jefferson Clinton occupied the White House then, much was made of the name. Then David displayed his passport, which showed that he also was named "William Clinton" (David being his middle name). The little place was nearly in an uproar. On another occasion, while Henry was there, he took me to lunch at a dockside restaurant in Honfleur. On a later day, he, David, and I drove to Bayeux, where General de Gaulle set foot again on French soil in 1944 and made his first post-landing speech (June 14). The cathedral, consecrated in 1077, is a splendid blend of Romanesque and Gothic styles. We visited also the museum which displays the famous embroidered cloth called the Tapestry of the Reine Mathilde (probably commissioned, however, not by Queen Mathilda, the wife of William the Conqueror, but by his half-brother, Bishop Odo of Bayeux). Nearly 70 meters in length, it illustrates events connected to the Norman conquest of England. War, war, century after century. We three then had lunch at the Lion d'Or. Photos taken afterward show a pair of men who appear to have enjoyed more than a little wine. Perhaps we needed escape from the students as much as they wanted time away from us.

We faculty members, and sometimes the students, were also invited by local residents to share their activities. At the Bastille Day celebration, held outdoors, loudspeakers played both "La Marseillaise" and "The Star-Spangled Banner," an indication of how Americans were appreciated in Normandy. Something went wrong, however: The solemn playing of the national anthems became somewhat farcical as the loudspeakers repeated them over and over. The ceremony was followed by a meal set up *al fresco* on long tables. That evening, a genteel couple of some years invited me to their house. On another occasion, a woman offered to take me to Caen to buy shoes (I had expressed the need for a new pair) and then, at my initiative, on a drive searching for a particular Norman town that, as I learned later, is in another area. These people could scarcely do enough for us. "*Ah, vous êtes américains*"—and the rest came as from a cornucopia. Whatever anti-Americanism visitors might find elsewhere in France in the 1990's, it was not discernible in Normandy. Yet these were the people whose towns had been blown up by the Allies in the battles of June 1944, who had perhaps seen death and destruction very close. They knew who had liberated them, however—English-speaking allies.

Are we called to be who and what we are (whether we live in freedom or not), to go where we find ourselves? Innumerable counterindications suggest that is not so: obstacles placed in our paths by circumstances and other people, which cause us to digress; false trails and obvious mismatches; dissatisfaction, failures, catastrophes, death. These may be called the interventions of fate. "*L'homme propose et Dieu dispose.*" Yet it is not clear that warning signs and suggested routes toward fulfillment of our potential do not exist; trails seem blazed, we recognize crumbs that we ourselves have dropped carelessly or strategically, we find ourselves on occasions exactly where we wish to be, or should be. True, chance plays an enormous role. When I was hired at Tulane, beginning in fall 1968, I was the third choice, two candidates having turned down the opportunity. To them I remain grateful. One declined to come unless his wife was given a tenured position in another department; that arrangement was deemed unsatisfactory. A second candidate met during his campus visit a certain faculty husband, a sour and aggressive man, who described aspects of New Orleans life in such a manner that the candidate was glad to remain in his California post. And so I was invited for an interview. Tulane suited me better than other universities would have, I believe, including three high-profile places where I was invited for interviews. The shape and color of my career henceforth (including the month at the abbey), as well as my daughter's life, have depended upon that nexus of chance, created by others' choices. But *my* choices also made it possible. "One must follow one's inclination," wrote Gide, "provided that it be upward."

Even if the undergraduates believed that their university, and within it the Normandy program, suited them well—by no means certain, though that's where they were—they were too inexperienced to sense a more vital fit, the sort that I could imagine. Such a fit is determined and created by time and the maturation of character, by self-revelation *via* searching, accepting, rejecting possibilities. Often it is understood after the fact, though with age one may come to recognize it at once, even anticipate it. That is where the vocation proves itself. Serendipity is not always serendipitous. As Hemingway suggested in *The Old Man and the Sea*, if you keep your line out and baited, you'll be ready for luck when luck comes. At their best, acts and situations are our children, planned or unplanned, made, often in joy, from our being, born to be our new realization in the world. (The reverse is also true: As Ferrante observes in Henry de Montherlant's splendid play *La Reine morte* [*Queen After Death*], a child is one of our acts, and thus cannot be denied.)

Recollections of the weeks spent in the abbey served me well, providing a reserve of understanding and tranquility on which I drew later that year, when there was unpleasantness for me at Tulane, in part the consequence of a foolish textbook choice (the book alluded to in "Literature and Its Contents") made while I was absent and imposed upon me, along with an awkward team-teaching arrangement. Unpleasantness arose also from the unwillingness of spoiled undergraduates to endure a rigorous course in French grammar, resentment on the part of a graduate assistant, from another continent, with a chip on her shoulder, and the poltroonery of a colleague and a dean. The architectural beauty, serenity, and order of the distant past, contrasted to what we knew of the imposed military occupation by the Reich in the 1940's and the violence of liberation in 1944—an image of historical struggle seen through Christian dialectics—had reinforced my sense of historical perspective and furnished reminders of the good. In the light of history, what were my differences with students and colleagues? Very little indeed. And I had been happy—not "imagined" as such, unlike the Sisyphus of Albert Camus, but truly so.

Bright Field

WITH FRIENDS, and a few figures whom I do not consider friends, I am in a fine house in uptown New Orleans. It's an evening party in December 1996. The occasion is a retirement celebration, my own. A fellow French professor, similarly about to end his teaching career, is the other guest of honor. The house, from the Victorian period but enlarged with a fine kitchen, casual room, and conservatory, is well suited to social gatherings, and the hosts' lovely furnishings and paintings, including an original work by Wifredo Lam, attract admiration.

The mood is cheerful; my colleague and I leave Tulane because we wish to (for different reasons). Whereas some facing retirement dread it, perhaps justly, having nothing useful to do, and others, or some of the same, do not flourish in their new condition—by life's irony, my poor father died shortly after having left his office for the last time, without having enjoyed his new leisure—I do not feel fate hanging over my head. Friends are glad for me. Those not friendly toward me smile a bit awkwardly or mumble a few commonplaces, but rejoice, quietly, over my departure; they will be freer to subvert tradition, common sense, and regulations, and eventually to substitute for rational curricular and degree arrangements their bizarre course designs founded on "critical thinking," sociological categories, and especially race/class/gender, with very little French literature involved—little poetry, in particular. Among the guests is a frizzy-haired dean, who, even on the rare "good hair day" in New Orleans, such as this one, looks as if she has just put her finger into a light socket. Even as she enjoys her free drinks and buffet dinner, she not only celebrates my leaving but also plots against a colleague of considerable international stature, who has had the misfortune to cross her. He and his wife are in fact the party hosts. During his remaining years at the university, he will be humiliated more than once.

Someone has turned on a pocket radio. Before iPhones and BlackBerries, this device allowed aficionados of updated news to keep abreast of things even when not at home and then interject the news into business talk or social events. (At least eyes did not remain glued to the radio, as if mesmerized, as with today's electronic handheld devices, among the most antisocial objects, and the most addictive, ever designed.) Why does someone want to hear news during a party? Even assuming such a wish, isn't it discourteous to turn aside from interlocutors for a private moment with the airwaves? Well, maybe the man went behind a potted palm. Anyhow, there is news indeed: An ocean-going vessel, the *Bright Field*, out of Hong Kong, fully loaded with grain, has just run into the riverfront on the east bank of the Mississippi, downtown, at the Riverwalk Marketplace, the site of shops and eateries and a classy condominium building.

Such accidents in the Port of New Orleans are not unusual, as attested by the apparent prosperity of numerous firms specializing in maritime law. The massive supports for the three bridges across the Mississippi, one of them called Huey P. Long after the man and the era, offer targets for wayward vessels. Algiers Point requires a very sharp turn. Barges lashed together and pushed by tugboats are weighty and cumbersome and can be lethal. Cargo ships and tankers should be less unpredictable; but what is predictable is the sometime partaking of alcohol by those at the wheel. Well before the *Bright Field* accident, a Greek ship ran aground a short distance upriver. Its horn bleated repeatedly, warning the levee to get out of the way. Alas, the levee did not move, and the captain, drunk (as later testimony showed), steered his ship into it. The collision of December 1996 was later ascribed by the Coast Guard to engine failure, a secondary cause being an inadequate automation system that produced warnings not constantly relayed to the master of the ship. That was another matter for the maritime attorneys to take up.

Meanwhile, at the retirement party we have a timely topic of conversation. What about the crew of the freighter, the residents who might have been in the garage or lobby of the posh condo building or those in the shops? The hosts are well acquainted with a couple who live there; they wonder about their friends' welfare. The talk buzzes. Sixty people, we will learn subsequently, have been injured; the ship has sustained damages of some $1,858,000, and the toll on land will be $15 million worth of damages.

Is the accident an omen of what is to come for me? To be sure, I am not superstitious, but only like the character in Fyodor Dostoevsky's *Underground Man*. (If memory serves, he says that he is too intelligent to be superstitious but is superstitious anyway.) In any case, the name *Bright Field* leads me to look ahead at the "field" on which I am about to embark, that of retirement, right at the turning of the year. Will it be bright? The name also recalls the fields of earlier life—endeavors, specialties—and beauties of the earth: fields of poppies in France seen from a train window and in paintings; plantings of corn and wheat in the Plains states; "fields" of cactus and greasewood stretching across the range to a far mesa, all shining in my mind with the light of happy memory.

Why had I chosen this retirement date? Why had my colleague similarly decided to say goodbye? Short of proven incompetence (and standards for judging such are notoriously lenient) or extreme moral turpitude (still more generous standards), the university could not, in practice, remove us from our positions; if I am not mistaken, federal law protected tenured faculty born after July 1, 1923, from mandatory retirement at any age. Daily existence could have been made difficult for me, but it was not; I had considerable support from most university officials, though not the frizzy-haired dean. I liked to work; overloads would not have discouraged me. (The lower administration, made up generally of poltroons, would not have dared impose them, anyhow; their spite would have been too obvious.) Increased committee assignments might have been a deterrent to staying on; but generally those who speak their mind, as I did, are less popular figures for committees than are sycophants. My fellow retiree, a likeable man somewhat older, had suffered a stroke a few years before; he'd been able to return to work and was glad to do so, but his strength had been sapped; eventually he and his wife returned to their Indiana home.

Political figures who are driven out of office, one way or another, aver, in order to save face, that they want to spend more time with friends and family. There was a grain of truth in that phrase for me. In calendar year 1996 I had seen my daughter, then a graduate student at Columbia, only two days. Surely not enough! To be sure, the year was not representative. We each were abroad for some months in connection with our respective undertakings, and our calendars did not match well: For nearly eight months, I had been in England, then on the Continent; as I returned to America, she was about to depart for an academic year in France. Still, even when we were both this side of the pond it was difficult to meet. In retirement, I expected to travel to New York more often and to visit friends elsewhere. In addition, I had numerous projects—a scholarly book (the study of French war literature pertinent to "In the Abbey"), translations of poems, and particularly my own poetry and creative prose. I was scheduled shortly to give lectures and readings in the southeast Atlantic states. I'd pursued similar projects while teaching, of course; but more time was needed. The fact that my final semester at the university was a difficult one, with a class of obstreperous, spoiled children, could not have been what inspired me to leave—the retirement decision had been made some months before—but added a flourish to the choice, a confirmation and seal. The outlook was bright, indeed.

Perhaps also I was ready for a challenge by way of change: a new life, a new routine, the need to exploit fully a different mode. I'd won at the poker games of academe, not the great pots, reserved for those of different character and interests from mine (ambitious administrators, the sycophants just mentioned, go-for-the-jugular types in the humanities, grant-getting researchers in the sciences), but very nice sums (so to speak); the antes were coming back to me amply. (And these gains were not taken from others, unlike true poker; nor was anyone *lésé*, generally. Contentment is like love: Though it expands, it does not reduce others', and may indeed increase theirs.) One should quit while one is ahead. It was the moment to experience a new existential field. "My field is time," said Goethe. Pindar suggested that one should "exhaust the field of the possible."

What is the field of the possible, today? Great gestures—renunciation of life, superhuman sacrifice? Not for me; I'm no saint, and extraordinary self-giving would be hard to arrange today (albeit not impossible). Exploration of the earth? It's already been mapped, and except for footnotes in the form of records ("the first woman to sail alone in a kayak the entire Missouri River" and so on), there's little to do. Cosmic travel? I'm far too old and afraid of heights. Politics? Ah, there's an idea. No particular training nor intellectual gifts are required; one's character need not be exceptional, at least not exceptionally solid or admirable; a bit of verbal facility is useful, and I've got it. Why not enter the lists, take on the field of challengers, defeat them all, and rise to heights of statesmanship? Well, there is no place now for statesmanship; it is not recognized, and to strive for it would be useless. Plenty of plums are there for the picking, however, in ordinary political ranks and activities. One must be qualified, however: dishonest, covetous, mendacious, crafty, full of guile (to use a biblical term), and ambitious beyond what I can imagine. Moreover, my approach, my views, my concerns and obvious indifference to numerous concerns of others would not appeal to many voters.

Perhaps I should go back to music, one of my girlhood loves, still possible, in theory. My training had ended, however. Can those in the Social Security crowd not only pick up where they left off but achieve new mastery of an instrument or their voice? Doubtless not. Or I could take up painting, about the history of which I know a great deal. I had never used a brush before, aware of my total lack of talent; but if one is a bit clever, no graphic talent is necessary now to make an artistic splash, especially for today's practitioners of installation "art" and similar creations, such as Christoph Büchel's: After having paid an average of $425 to New York area homeless people for their shopping carts filled with their goods, he installed them around Frieze New York (an art fair centered on contemporary work) and offered them to collectors for prices ranging from $35,000 to $50,000.

One way to make an impression would be to commit outstanding crimes or start a great conflagration, morally or literally. This method is as old as Erostratus, who set fire to the temple at Ephesus as a way of making himself immortal. That the act was committed, it is said, on the very night Alexander the Great was born is a footnote. That, in order to counter his ambition, the Ephesians forbade anyone to utter his name is psychology; the more it was forbidden, the more famous he became. Maximilien de Robespierre too carried out unusual deeds, changed things, and is remembered, just as, on a smaller scale, is Lee Harvey Oswald. I could take a semiautomatic rifle and fire away in a mall, a school, an office building. But I don't know how to shoot such a weapon; and since so many others carry out similar acts in the course of a decade, I would scarcely be viewed as a high achiever. Nor have I spent the better part of my adulthood pursuing humane values—truth, beauty, honesty, and even a kind of intellectual goodness and everyday morality—and leading others to cultivate them, only to destroy human beings capable of recognizing and appreciating them.

In fact, standards for the most outstanding and memorable crimes would be hard to meet. The greatest criminals of the 20th century are remembered well—Joseph Stalin, Pol Pot (both of whom attacked their own people), Adolf Hitler (who persecuted mainly those he viewed as aliens)—but, with a few exceptions, the names of their henchmen, even the worst, are no longer current. This is one aspect of what Hannah Arendt called the banality of evil. Richard Reid, the "shoe bomber," is still remembered in America and the United Kingdom, perhaps because he has an Occidental name, but the "panty bomber" of Detroit has become anonymous, identified only by his underwear.

So, what in fact shall I do? Nothing striking, still less revolutionary. As I project the future, I shall continue with what I did before, with some exceptions, and with greater concentration in certain cases. Character does not change; it was molded, and it is set. A certain injection of intellectual and real vagabondage will now be possible, however, and may allow for new initiatives. I shall write poetry, essays, criticism, and fiction, read, travel, lecture, see friends and family, both in the city where I live and elsewhere. I'll go to France and England regularly and, in due course, pay visits, as yet unplanned, to the Virgin Islands, South America, Sicily, Holland, Sweden, Austria, Wales, Scotland, Ireland, and Mediterranean and Oriental ports. I'll travel in various parts of the United States more frequently. In the first few years of my retirement, at least, I'll manage, as planned, to see often and enjoy the company of my daughter, married shortly thereafter and with children some years later. New friends, whom I shall regard highly, will appear on the horizon, both in Europe and America. This is to say that I'll cultivate what the ancients valued so highly, friendship. Giving to the word *charity*, I trust, some of its genuine meaning as a theological virtue, I shall devote time to others, less eleemosynary bodies than individuals at hand with their various needs. Thus I shall act as a factotum for someone long dependent upon me, visit the elderly, help former students as they recast their dissertations to create articles, write recommendations for them, comment on poems submitted for my opinion, "visit prisoners" (one, by means of letters), volunteer (in intellectual matters only).

What will I miss from my teaching career as a whole and especially from the last decade or so at Tulane? Capricious administrators, vexing colleagues—often indolent, sometimes arrogant—whining students, tedious committee meetings, committee reports to write that subsequently are filed away unnoticed? Well, after a camping trip, does one miss mosquitoes, chiggers, gnats? I shan't miss advising freshmen, as sometimes I was assigned to do. ("Dr. Brosman, should I take Psychology 102 or Astronomy 101 ['Astronomy for Poets']?"—how could I possibly put myself in that student's mind?) I won't pine for inspectors, miscellaneous Buttinskies, and visiting lecturers—they were usually not very good. I won't regret not being present for the heralding of the latest pedagogical innovations (insubstantial puffs, if not downright harmful) nor being obliged to help implement them. Nor dealing with students who appear, a few days before the semester ends, to inquire about turning in late papers, taking the final at a later date, not taking it at all, and so forth.

Those were the mosquitoes. It would be foolish to rage against them, even to dwell much on them. I did have (so to speak) insecticide, in various forms. And once the vexations cease, one does not feel them, except to regret that so much good time was wasted thereby. Perhaps even it served, indirectly (as the grit and water of life's tumbler do). ("They also serve who only stand and wait.") Might the uses of such adversity prove to be sweet, as time works itself out? My reserves of understanding and serenity grew, certainly. As Ruth McEnery Stuart, a Louisiana author, wrote, "The landscape needs its clouds to give value to the blue."

Forty years of academic camping at various institutions did provide much to be savored at the time and retrospectively. I'll miss the students—the real ones, in the proper sense of the term. Ah, the light in the student's eye when he solves a grammatical mystery, recognizing, for instance, that what appears to be a pleonastic *ne* is in fact a true negation! And notes such as that left in my mailbox shortly before Christmas by one Alice, a graduate student in my Proust seminar, as she emerged from a rabbit hole of surprises and challenges: "It was hard, but it was wonderful. Thank you." My pedagogical instinct being what it is, since I have no more pupils on the benches, my poor friends will find themselves acting as stand-ins and get elements of lectures and guidance that they may not wish for.

I'll occasionally think of what is supposed to be and sometimes is the fruitful exchange of information and views among colleagues and graduate students, the sort that affords insight or spurs one on. I'll recall the pleasures of campus friendships, the good news about friends' publications, the in-house lecture series I ran for a few years with papers by graduate students and faculty. I'll think of my doctoral students now working in Louisiana universities and elsewhere. It will be a pleasure to remember the 3.998 average achieved by one of our students, with a triple major, who carried off the prize for the top graduate.

And the parties! The "Frogs" were known for having frequent and very good gatherings, often on a Friday afternoon, with French wine and cheeses, of course. In 1988 the Modern Language Association (an organization that I quit upon retirement) held its national meeting in New Orleans. A generous publisher gave me funds to hold an invitation-only reception on an upper floor of the Napoleon House in the French Quarter. Word traveled by oral telephone; the place was mobbed, and the policeman we'd hired as security was barely able to stop crashers from making their way upstairs.

In the nearly score of years since my retirement, what was projected has indeed been fulfilled. Readers will be spared any detailing of these undertakings. They may not appear much. No new worlds conquered, though marriage with Patric after we became acquainted again is surely an exceptional sentimental adventure, the joys of which still sparkle for us each day. But what is life—is it not fundamentally similar no matter where it is carried out? What is true human achievement? No man, no woman is capable of going beyond his human data and his circumscription; only saints may surpass, briefly, their condition.

Thus my current flow of life resembles the past, while being different, and resembles others'. In the light of history, what were my differences with students and colleagues? Very little indeed. To return to an earlier metaphor, I perceive that, in a way, I have camped my way through life. The sojourning was prolonged and serious (if not enforced), but was still a temporary enterprise (of course!) that did not seem to be the entirety of experience—more a shoot off the trunk, a branch of the main line, not quite identified. As a child I had intimations of another reality around me, not constant but, rather, intermittent—something of an aura, I suppose. That sense of another reality receded gradually and departed, replaced by the praxis of responsibility, but the memory can be glimpsed occasionally at the edges of consciousness. It is not a question of a mystical experience—certainly not—but it suggests why for years I have been interested in embodiment, as numerous poems of mine show. No undertaking is ever one's whole life, notwithstanding familiar talk to the contrary; life cannot be reduced to deeds or situation but instead goes beyond its boundaries toward projected being—that is, until at the end no further surpassing of the embodied situation is possible, and what is here is all there will be here.

The party has ended; saying long Creole goodbyes, we make our way out, tying little knots of conversation on the thread of evening. The sky is truly a bright field tonight; New Orleans is not so large nor so brilliantly lit along its uptown streets that, on a crisp evening, stars are lost in the darkness. So I set out on the river of the new year and a new status, with considerable cargo and lots of ports at which to call. Will I lose power, sink or run into a levee, be salvaged and renamed, and sail the high seas again (as the ship has done, under two different names)? Better, we generally think, not to know our future, inscribed for us somewhere perhaps—in our own selves, even—but in a language we do not know. To see in advance would create dread, were the images awful, or impatience, should they be good. All I knew was that, in the sense of "well-being," I had been happy. I do not boast of this. Though Aristotle found reasonable the traditional advice to count no man happy until he dies, he saw that happiness truly existed, connected, of course, to character, and that one could legitimately say of someone, "He was happy." May it continue, with occasional spurs of discontent. As Alain (Emile Chartier), a 20th-century French philosopher and pedagogue, wrote, "Happiness supposes always, doubtless, some concern, some passion, a *pointe* of pain which awakens us to ourselves."

O Literature, Thou Art Sick: The Consequences of Theory

THE PRESENT CONDITION OF LITERATURE (as that term is ordinarily understood), at least in America, is obviously unhealthy. Its illness is owing not only to internal undermining, "the invisible worm" of William Blake's "The Sick Rose," but also to external conditions, the "howling storm" on which the worm (however implausibly) rode. External and internal decline, all too visible in this case, go together, of course. While they can be traced partly to the enormous social and cultural changes of previous centuries, they are principally a mid- and late-20th-century development, reaching into the 21st century, involving separation (or "alienation") of good readers from good writers, then decreasing numbers of both. Earlier, *belles-lettres* were meaningful, as well as vigorous and popular, on both sides of the Atlantic. In 19th-century France, Lamartine could reply to a detractor that his new book of verse would soon be in every cobbler's pocket. The poems of Victor Hugo, from his odes at age 20 to *The Art of Being a Grandfather*, 55 years later, were read widely, not of course by those with no schooling, but often by those with little. His serialized novels had vast audiences, and not just in Europe; American poet and critic Morris Bishop told how his father's family waited impatiently for each new episode to arrive in the mail. Now, in contrast, poetry no longer belongs to the mainstream, as Dana Gioia observed, too gently, some years ago in the *Atlantic Monthly*, and fiction has been largely degraded.

Among contemporary conditions favoring the decline of literature, in addition to critical theory (to be discussed shortly), are the dominance of popular culture, low moral standards, and erosion of language (all connected, all pertinent to the degraded standards of *The New Yorker*, sketched earlier). Popular culture, spread by every medium, drives out better creations, as, according to Gresham's Law, inferior products, if they reach critical mass, usually do to superior ones. Instead of being confined to undiscriminating readers, like dime novels or what the French call "train station literature," inferior writing has usurped the place of good in the marketplace and is even admired by some who should know better. Such vulgarized writing is now the principal, sometimes the only, concern of countless editors and publishers (the latter, with exceptions, large conglomerates uninterested in quality).

Popular culture has been legitimized, placed on a footing with, or rather elevated above, high culture; at a local state university a course on rock 'n' roll is accepted for elective credit in a liberal-arts curriculum that has, in contrast, no foreign-language requirement. (Far more offensive examples could be cited.) Certain critics attack explicitly anything referring to past literary or other cultural products. Low moral standards allow for the crudest material to enrich its creators, even—in the case of so-called art—be subsidized by tax dollars, through moral indifference or, worse, as direct defiance, and without any acknowledgment that such degradation is a violation of human dignity. As for language standards, consider what you hear from television news. Even *The New Yorker*, once known for its rigorous standards of English (as well as its fact-checking), now allows its journalists (as readers know) to use routinely such barbarisms as "It is *him*." Maybe even the editors don't know better. To ungrammatical language is added the filthy talk that used to be associated with fishwives and sailors. The meaning of words is so adulterated that the word *artist* is now applied to such as Britney Spears and Michael Jackson. Style, in the sense of *good style*, has been so devalued that those who esteem it are condemned as offensive snobs. Though novelists, playwrights, and poets can blame society for abandoning standards of good taste and the ideal of lasting literary value, they too are responsible, as they adopt shamelessly the worst demands of publishers or producers; look at Larry McMurtry, more gifted and a better craftsman than one would suppose from some of his products.

Others who have sabotaged literature are the critical theorists. Now, theory need not be a literary Fifth Column. For instance, *Theory of Literature* (1949) by René Wellek and Austin Warren had as its aim not dismantling literature but clarifying literary values and what can be known of the creative process, along with proposing strategies for analysis and judgment; and while certain approaches there reflected changed modes of thinking, masterworks remained honored, not undermined. Well over half of Hazard Adams's massive anthology *Critical Theory Since Plato* (1971) is devoted to canonic critics who wrote generally in support of the literary enterprise, though a few might be surprised to see how their thought has been interpreted. In contrast, Adams's and Leroy Searle's 1986 anthology, *Critical Theory Since 1965*, includes mostly contemporary writers hostile to conventional literature, many of them foreign thinkers who directed their critical aggression against America (while often accepting her dollars). Here, the word *critical* no longer refers to "criticism" in the broad sense, as Aristotle, Horace, Sir Philip Sidney, Joseph Addison, Friedrich Schlegel, Samuel Taylor Coleridge, and innumerable others practiced it, but, chiefly, to radical cultural critique (hence the proximity of "cultural theory" and "critical theory") and deconstruction based on revisionist history, linguistics, sociology, and other disciplines in their postmodern stages. Therein lies the difficulty.

What is meant by the term *postmodernism* can be defined roughly, with respect to literary criticism, as denying, on several grounds, first, the claims of standard, nonradicalized literature to *prima facie* truth and meaning; next, values of taste and beauty; and, third, the worth of writing from privileged groups, considered oppressive.

The first of these positions depends on denying the indicative functions of language as previously assumed (more or less). This denial is the principal postmodernist claim. The writers of the canon and their readers knew that words stand for realities. Milton quoted Cicero's statement that "names are truly the signs of things." The towering writers of the early 20th century, such as Eliot, Yeats, and Proust, and many less celebrated figures, such as Marianne Moore and William Carlos Williams, still believed in words and their connection to the real; new ways of employing language were still art and were valuable. Proust believed *only* in words. The meaning of a work could be chiefly its beauty, or its truth, or both; it could be lyrical, dramatic, narrative, meditative, satirical; but it was still meaning. Even the Surrealists believed in language. The "tradition" was honored, if obliquely.

That recognition was, however, still predicated on the function of language as conveyer of meaning: Words meant what they said, even if antiphrastically; whereas the strain of postmodern criticism for which the late Jacques Derrida deserves credit, along with long-deceased linguist Ferdinand de Saussure, denies the capacity of language to hold and transmit meaning. Words are unstable, indeterminate, without intrinsic connection to what they stand for, and always defined by other words; all statements can always be deconstructed as contradictory, untenable. (Belief in the Word is obviously excluded.) Perfect logic cannot be achieved in language (the old Cratylist complaint or Cretan liar's paradox, illustrated by the paradox "All statements are false"). Meaning is always in the future, endlessly deferred, by what Derrida called *différance*.

Derrida denied, by the way, the near-nihilism that his position constituted. Shortly before he died, he said that philosophy had been for him "the search for an ethos and a way of life." However lofty that aim may sound, his influence was nonetheless nefarious. That anyone should read philosophy or literature or anything at all, except for the pleasure of deconstructing it, contradicts his postmodern theses, of course. But the latter constitute obviously an impracticable extreme, a *meta-criticism* (as he might say); even he used words to question them. In practice, his denunciation of the power of language to denote the real and the true is, along with other theories, called into service normally to attack the truth-value of canonic literary and philosophic works, not language as used in daily life: It can be presumed that Derrideans not in good health still take their blood-pressure medicine according to the dose as indicated on the package.

Furthermore, since all writing consists of words used by others and thus relates to other texts in an endless pool of intertextuality, the writer is merely making waves, reshuffling no one's material. There is no authority; there is no author. If you add a further assertion—familiar since Sigmund Freud's ideas were popularized, alas, in Europe and America—to the effect that the self is not only in perpetual conflict but the plaything of unconscious, uncontrollable drives, and thus is not the rational, aware being that would engage in controlled literary creation, you have all you need to question the value of literature as it was heretofore understood.

Or almost everything. For there is also the multiculturalist claim that Occidental literature must be rejected because of its privileged social origins and practice. (The postmodernists do not use much ink attacking the values of taste and beauty; they are elitist and thus rejected *ipso facto* along with social privilege.) This claim derives from what Richard Weaver called *presentism*—the filtering ideological vision of today. The "Dead White Male," whose products are racist, sexist, often nationalist, elitist, rationalist (analytical, "vertical" rather than "horizontal"), and deliberately oppressive (whether such oppressors knew it or not), and who excluded the "marginalized" except in rare circumstances, is a monster who, having terrorized the past, must now be slain. Since one blow does not suffice, the attacks remain ongoing. Four veins of thought (all well represented in the Adams-Searle anthology) have contributed to this new dogma: Marxism, with its theory of social classes and economic exploitation; post-Marxism, which adds to economic and class theory that of the formative, oppressive role of cultural products, structures, and institutions (Michel Foucault's credo); radical feminism, with its hatred of male achievements and deliberate discounting of historical conditions that shaped past customs; and postcolonialism, with its victimology and resentment of the West. According to enthusiasts of this thinking, the literature that originated among and was practiced by those in power is necessarily oppressive and "inauthentic," as Marxists would say. Aesthetic criteria and values are rejected; refined style is deemed exclusionary, false; good taste constitutes shackles. Even the venerable genres are viewed as tyrannical. Only new writing, by those who denounce analytic reason and adopt an adversarial relationship to past or present (such figures include postcolonials and other dark-skinned peoples, women, prisoners, homosexuals and other deviants, and the acolytes of all of these), is viewed as legitimate. There is something of a split here between the postmodern vein and a more socially directed critical theory based on multiculturalism. Those who believe the world can be changed by writing—the old-style revolutionaries and new activists—part company with those more radical thinkers who question the efficacy of language.

Enthusiasts may assert that, whether critical or creative, the new multiculturalist writing constitutes a valuable creative *élan*. Just as earlier generations pushed the boundaries, "negated the tradition," or, as earlier I quoted Cocteau saying, tried to see "just how far you can go too far," the formerly marginalized and their apologists, the new critical theorists, push back the frontiers; they are literature's astronauts. Perhaps. Certainly, from the Greeks on, writers have displeased traditionalists by breaking molds, and daring products of literary evolution may, after a period of incomprehension, be viewed as masterpieces rather than provocations. Euripides overturned certain conventions of his predecessors and was considered disturbing. Victor Hugo shocked critics by dividing, through caesuras, the alexandrine line of twelve syllables into three groups (4/4/4) instead of the usual two (6/6). His innovations in fiction and on the stage—scenes by torchlight, amours between a servant and a noble, characters of grotesque physique or monstrous soul—were deemed still worse. Flaubert was put on trial for *Madame Bovary*; certain poems by Baudelaire were condemned in court and the author fined. No matter: Romanticism assimilated these innovations and disturbing materials and countless others until they too became literary commonplaces and were extended or replaced. Current critical theory is different in kind, however, since it, first, denies value *ipso facto* to creations by members of condemned groups (or holding forbidden views—think of how Eliot is regarded by cultural critics); second, subverts belief in truth and meaning by challenging the ability of words to refer to and convey, in any sense, the real; third, attacks values of taste and beauty; and, fourth, undermines the ideal of the learned man. The last enterprise may be the worst, since, if armed with learning, one could see through the others.

The most deplorable thing is that, in the general removal of literary culture from the public forum (there are hardly any independent critics nowadays), these critical sophists have come to dominate the academy, which is the locus of any such literary education as American youth get. Postmodern thinking appears to have filtered down to many high schools, and no university offering graduate studies in literature is without courses in critical theory, supported sometimes by a disproportionate number of faculty positions, plus lectures and workshops. One wonders, nevertheless, how many students and even faculty read the turgid prose of its practitioners, which at its worst is gibberish (well, some of my graduate students did not read assignments given by colleagues, I know). There are further consequences. Since analytical thinking, the characteristic mode of Occidental men, is considered oppressive, and organizing literary study by language or territorial division reflects, it is asserted, oppressive structures and "opaque" social relationships, there has been a concerted effort to break down departments, curricula, and syllabi organized rationally (by language, genre, or chronology). Anyone can teach almost anything, preferably something unconventional, in any context. A Wesleyan University (Connecticut) faculty member recalled in *The American Scholar* (Winter 2005) that one student was assigned Toni Morrison's *Beloved* in all four courses he took one semester. Chronology is especially despised—a symptom of postmodernist scorn for history; dates are viewed as irrelevant. When students objected, on grounds of historical usage, to a famous professor's sexual interpretation of the word *screw* in an Emily Dickinson poem, he retorted that the author's meaning was immaterial.

Not all contemporary modes of criticism are so destructive as what has been sketched here; certain approaches, such as narratology (a way of analyzing plot) and reader-response criticism—emphasizing the context of reading—extend commonsensical understandings from the past, which, rephrased and refocused by discerning critics, may lead to a finer understanding of how literature works. They are tools, not dogma. Restating that which "oft was thought" in an altered light can be useful. Circumstances have changed; there are new readers, new works, and new ways of looking at old ones. But denying the foundations of past achievements is unjustified. And no criticism should take the place of the literature it is supposed to serve. The reading lists of the past have not only been revised; they have, in some quarters, nearly given way to criticism on authors once read firsthand. Critical theorists are something of a priestly caste, holding arcane secrets, with the power to validate or invalidate our reading. If we can be initiated into their obscure jargon, we too can penetrate their esoteric truths and be saved.

Literature still matters, nevertheless, and its American audience, though small, could be cultivated and enlarged by proper curricula in colleges and devoted publishers. Its traditional uses and pleasures ("*plaire et instruire*," wrote Nicolas Boileau in his *Art poétique*, following Horace) remain valid. To portray, examine, and reflect on life, in general terms (as done by the most philosophic writers) or from the individual viewpoint (the more characteristic literary approach); to enrich experience or add to it; to propose ways of being, seeing, knowing; to offer justification and judgment, especially warnings against self-infatuation, and explore the possibility of the moral life—those have been the functions of good writing since the Greeks replaced myth, which functioned somewhat similarly, by rigorously formal, highly reflective modes. By requiring shaping, condensing, focusing, reflection, literature stylizes life, multiplies it, and broadens understanding of ourselves and others, whose innermost emotional and intellectual experiences are made available to us. (To know them thus is voyeurism only to those who make it so; properly, it is sharing in their humanity.)

Good taste is not, of course, always imperative. Was Rabelais refined? Is the Porter's scene in *Macbeth* in good taste? As I argued in an earlier essay here, the coarse, along with the delicate, and evil, with good, are part of the real and thus of literature; but in the Occidental literary tradition the offensive is not a model, and corrective values are always visible, sometimes juxtaposed. To wallow in disgust and invite others to do so cannot be the purpose of literature. As Chilton Williamson, Jr., pointed out in his review (*Chronicles: A Magazine of American Culture*, April 2006) of Cormac McCarthy's *No Country for Old Men*, even McCarthy, often the painter of the most depraved, the least redeemed of human beings, works into his novels a moral dimension, barely glimpsed but thereby all the more crucial.

Literature always points to something beyond itself, a pleasure, verity, judgment, vision. It is more than rewarding; it is essential. The modernists recognized these truths. Stevens observed, "The pleasure of poetry is to contribute to man's happiness." Williams, in one of his last poems, "Asphodel, That Greeny Flower," wrote that it was hard "to get the news from poems":

> yet men die miserably every day
> for lack
> of what is found there.

Richard Eberhart said in a 1968 speech: "The point of poetry is to make meanings for your life, to discover durable truth of yourself within the flux of life and time . . . Poetry defends the inner capacities of man."

Belles lettres can make another contribution: Rigor in language both reflects and leads to rigor of thought, surely an urgent national need. That is, reading the best of what has been written cultivates discrimination. Consider the gullibility of the American audience and today's cultural fare, which the media reinforce or create: government pronouncements, "studies" (sociological, psychological, quasimedical, all purportedly scientific), commercial advertising, tendentious publicity and undertakings of not-for-profits, including universities and museums, live drama, film, reinforced and publicized by print journalism and television. What is at face value information with the presumption of truth or, in the case of entertainment, is taken as normative is, in fact, frequently misleading (often deliberately), manipulative, corruptive. The cultivation of good literature now and the study of great works of the past (along with philosophy and history) could provide means to identify and resist what is false and depraved. Perhaps Ezra Pound, Vorticist, crank, asylum inmate, but wise in this respect, should have the last word: "If a nation's literature declines, the nation atrophies and declines."

Stones

NOT FANCIFUL NOR EYE-CATCHING, the word barely draws you in, though it does suggest what is solid, firm, dense. That's what I like about stones—the solidity, the certainty, the lack of pretense. They are what they are, neither more nor less; it is we human beings who see qualities and potentiality in them—utility, hardness, impediment, beauty, ugliness. Many stones are indeed very ordinary. Others, unexceptional on the outside, conceal gorgeous crystal interiors. Still others, unlike geodes, conceal nothing (some *are concealed*, originally); but their potentiality is enormous, at least for the craftsman or artist (stonemason, sculptor, architect, engraver, landscaper, jeweler) who sees his idea emerge from their crude natural forms. Think of splendid gemstones, dug from earth's dark veins, and others, semi-precious, such as turquoise, jade, obsidian. For Shakespeare, in *Richard II*, England was "this precious stone set in the silver sea." But in their natural state, gems present themselves without affectation. If anything, stones may be too modest, except when faceted and displayed by a woman of taste or a jeweler—perhaps on black or midnight-blue velvet—where their brilliant, pure simplicity and their color, in the case of rubies and emeralds, outshine everything else (nor would the price be modest, in that case). Even then, their presence is quiet, tasteful. Fine jewelry stores are rarely riotous; prospective buyers and the sales staff alike maintain even and respectful tones of voice, except for an occasional exclamation of admiration escaping a buyer or, more likely, the woman for whom a gift has been chosen.

As a girl, I spent as much time as possible in the high territory of the Rocky Mountains, where the soil and mountainsides do not belie the name. Driving out of Denver, one met, near Morrison, the Red Rocks, including an amphitheater for musical and dramatic performances. This chain of immense red sandstone formations continues down the Front Range and becomes, in Colorado Springs, the enchanting Garden of the Gods. I loved arriving at the Red Rocks, for their beauty and their role as heralds of what was to come. Somewhat higher, along a hogback, we could see, on uplifted sedimentary rock, the huge fossilized footprints of dinosaurs. (My cousin Jean believed that, despite the epidemic of vandalism, a national disease, the fossils have not been destroyed nor removed to a museum.) After further ascents, we crossed Kenosha Pass to go to my grandmother's cabin near

Deckers. This small weekend and summer place, surrounded by pine and spruce (hence a lovely carpet of needles), was on a hillside with numerous smooth boulders; the cabin even backed up to a rather flat one, wonderful for play. In the soil there were abundant rocks, both igneous and sedimentary. Farther south, outside Woodland Park, the same mountain landscape surrounded the ranger station and its residence, where my uncle and aunt, my mother's sister, presided.

My lifelong taste for the lithic may date from those summer weeks. My grandfather's gift of a boxed set of minerals illustrating the Mohs hardness scale fortified this liking. (Long before Friedrich Mohs, Theophrastus and Pliny the Elder had compared minerals by their hardness.) Grandfather gave me likewise a larger box, made of fine wood, displaying samples of many kinds of rock and ore. In the Girl Scouts, one of the interests I pursued was, not surprisingly, geology. My family's move to the Big Bend afforded chances to enlarge my acquaintance with rocks and soils and formations of aesthetic and geological interest. Did I want specimens? I had only to step out, not to the back garden, which my father kept in good grass (a small "Green Park," like that in London—no flowers), but just beyond the inner fence; dozens of types, even geodes, awaited me, scattered on the unimproved terrain. Contrast this experience with my daughter's. Born and reared in New Orleans, she could find by digging only small bits of gravel and occasional shells. (This was on what had been plantation land, then someone's side garden, until 1963.) When she was 11, she and I took the Trailways bus (her father not allowing her to fly) from New Orleans to Colorado. We stopped with my cousins Beth and Jim Phillips, who had a good collection of geodes and, in addition, a rocky garden. Kate was so enchanted by the rocks she was allowed to dig that she wanted to take back a sackful (an impractical proposal). You can love what you once had; you can love what you didn't have.

If one wants to test the drawing power of boulders and rock formations, Colorado offers fine opportunities. At the New Mexico border, take the Cumbres & Toltec Scenic Railway, an old narrow-gauge line, and you will pass through cuts that show rock of different origins and times—cuts so narrow that they remind me of those medieval streets in Europe (there are some in colonial Mexican cities also) where you can almost touch both sides at a time. Or travel over Spring Creek Pass and Slumgullion Pass, in the San Juan Mountains, to admire huge rock facings as well as taluses covered with scree. There and elsewhere in the area one has a wide variety of mineral matter, whether breccia (hot volcanic ash that covered older rock, as at Vesuvius), sedimentary layers, glacial till, petrified mud, layered volcanic ash, or spreads of igneous rock that would deserve the name *el Malpaís*, as various igneous fields in New Mexico are called, including the Jornado del Muerto, or Day's Journey of the Dead Man.

The utility of lithic material was exploited, of course, hundreds of thousands of years ago. I think of the earliest Stone Age, when men lived in caves (openings in the rock), used stones, not yet chipped and shaped, as crude weapons, and made fire rings. (Fire and rock are related; we recall that Prometheus, the Titan, was chained to a rock for having given out the secret of fire.) The connection between stone and art dates from this early period (small sculptures and monumental paintings on cave walls). Spiritual power was ascribed to stone by many peoples, including the Celts and, much more recently, the Anasazi, who, respectively, constructed circles of vertical boulders and stone kivas, the meanings mysterious but connected in some cases to the summer solstice. (The architects of the mountaintop basilica at Vézelay—the largest Romanesque edifice in France, the stones of which were hauled up by hand—similarly designed the nave with the summer and winter solstices in mind, so that particular and symbolic light effects are created at midday on those dates.) Stone later became a means of writing, as both tablet and stylus; the decipherment of the Rosetta Stone by Thomas Young and Jean-François Champollion made that piece of black stone famous. The greatest arts of ancient civilizations, as we know them, were those of architecture and ornamentation; most of the Seven Wonders of the Ancient World involved stone.

Stones and rock are everywhere in the English poetic tradition, from Shakespeare (Othello's heart turned to stone), to Wordsworth's "violet by a mossy stone" and "Rolled round in earth's diurnal course, / With rocks, and stones, and trees," to the "cold gray stones" of Tennyson's sea and Eliot's "Here is no water but only rock." Stones are frequently present in my poetry, usually with a positive association, as in poems concerning churches. In "Tres Hermanas" I wrote of "the strange mothering of stones." If earth is imagined as a female deity, then stone, the most lasting feature of the soil and landscape, must have a place in this maternal representation. Burial is a return to mother earth. The appeal of gravestones is powerful, marking in solid material both dissolution of the more fragile body and its duration in memory. That old grave markers become pocked, often lichen-covered, and the letters illegible adds to the pathos of churchyards: Even stone does not endure, nor does memory, for that matter. Of the mighty stone works of Ozymandias there remains only a "colossal wreck."

The difference between rock and stone is, of course, chiefly semantic, not geological. The categories of substances to which the words refer are fundamentally the same, with considerable overlapping but distinctions also; in all uses, we know what we mean. (Derrida's views on language have already been examined and rejected earlier in this volume.) English has numerous other lexical items in the group. French is likewise semantically rich. One says "*une pierre*" for a building block or a pebble or stone held in the hand, or "*un caillou*" for such a pebble; one speaks also of "*de la pierre*" for the substance in general or the material of a particular object; but there's also "*du rocher*" (of rock, made of rock) and "*un rocher*" / "*des rochers*" (a large rock, boulders), as well as "*du gravier*" (gravel). Then there is the word *pierreries*, for precious stones. There are also proper names—Pierre, Pierrette, Pierrot (nickname, and the character from the Commedia dell'Arte).

The valence of stones changes in our imagination and our literary and moral tradition, as in history. The worth of the object is reflected, to some degree, in the choice of term. *Stone* is often negative, *rock* positive. "X has a heart of stone," but "Y is a rock." Niobe, having been at first "all tears" from grief, becomes stone, and Medusa turns to stone all those who look directly on her. One becomes *petrified* with fear. Stone is inhumane. "Z has a stony gaze." Obviously, stones are connected to prisons, as in "Stone walls do not a prison make." Jean-Paul Sartre's antihero in *La Nausée* picks up pebbles on the beach and skips them across the water, not in admiration but in pure ennui, tinged with a bit of disgust because the pebbles have damp sand or mud clinging to them. One of Samuel Beckett's characters, an *obsessionnel*, transfers stones from one pocket to another. As in Eliot's phrase, stones are often opposed to water, the solid to the flowing, the sterile to the life-giving; but in the case of river stones, worn to smooth texture and rounded by the stream of time, there seems to be almost a wedding of the liquid and the solid. And "dripping water hollows stone," according to Lucretius and many followers. In Judeo-Christian scripture, the connotation of *stone* is often negative. The angels shall have charge of the righteous man, lest he dash his foot against a stone. If a son asks for bread, will his father give him a stone? "He that is without sin among you, let him first cast a stone." Christ was enclosed in a tomb of stone; then when the angel rolled away the stone, its power, standing for that of death, vanished.

Rock, in contrast, is foundation. "The Lord is my rock, and my fortress." "Thou art my rock, and my salvation." "Rock of Ages, cleft for me . . . " The apostle Simon becomes Peter the Rock, on whom the house, or the Church (the Body), will be built. The image then is one of immense solidity, like that of the pyramids (built precisely to give such an image) and, in nature, Gibraltar and, closer to home, Shiprock, the giant basalt formation in New Mexico. Rock is thus life. When Moses and Aaron spoke to the rock and Moses struck it, water flowed. Yet this life-giving rock is not necessarily shelter. As one of various similar songs, based on the Epistle to the Hebrews (chapter six), puts it:

No hidin' place down there;
no hidin' place down there.
Run to the rock to hide my face;
rock cried out "No hiding place";
no hidin' place down there.

Because stones are rock seen as, or turned into, material for use, they are—despite negative valences often—what constitutes the human dimension of the substance. That is, they have potentiality, lending themselves to human creativity; they are opportunity. Or they demonstrate their value by being already transformed into walkways, walls, edifices, decorative objects. Marble is not only a favored material but a stock image of lithic characteristics—hard, cold, yet beautiful and suitable for sculpting. It suggests luxury, wealth—that is, culture beyond the fulfilling of basic needs. Although, in slang, gems are "rocks," they are normally called stones, as are pieces of rock used in exchange (wampum). Stone is also the ur-altar, the place of sacrifice, from Isaac to Mithraic killings of the bull to Iphigeneia to Christian rite. *Rock* remains ordinarily the original stuff, beautiful, solid, more permanent than we, certainly. But, as I noted, we see *stone* (possibility) in *rock*. As Pat and I traveled through the stunning areas I mentioned earlier, we said to each other repeatedly, "A sculptor would see that as a statue in waiting." Through erosion, nature had already done considerable sculpting. We also noted that a mild earthquake would bring down tons of material and redesign the landscape.

Stone is assimilable to human beings themselves: "*Je ne bastis que pierres vives; ce sont hommes*," wrote Rabelais. The meaning may be even theological. From the Psalms and then Saint Matthew's Gospel comes the finely imagined phrase (because it expresses the dialectical reversal of given values that underlies Christian thought, as in *felix culpa*): "The stone which the builders refused is become the head stone of the corner." In the Gospel according to Saint Luke, Jesus says, when the Pharisees ask Him to rebuke His disciples, "If these should hold their peace, the stones would immediately cry out." It is appropriate that the highest expression of lithic potentiality is in ecclesiastical architecture and ornamentation. For *The Stones of Venice*, Ruskin's detailed investigation of architectural principles as carried out in the Veneto, he studied 80 different churches. In the Romanesque and early Gothic styles, stone is both itself and other; it is transformed without losing its rocky character. (By the time the great Baroque edifices were erected, Saint Peter's in Rome being the supreme example, the resemblance with natural formations—that is, the primitive quality—was lost.)

Certain little chapels, tucked in at the side of the road, resemble rock formations. The Carolingian Oratory of Germiny-des-Prés in the Loiret (not to be confused with the Paris Romanesque church of almost the same name) and the great Romanesque basilicas and Gothic cathedrals often share features with nature, their modest or imposing flanks, apses and side chapels, rough texture, and uneven shape, with curious ornamentation, whether lofty or grotesque, corresponding to cliffs, rock façades, and palisades. A favorite of mine is the church St.-Just de Valcabrère ("Goat Valley"), built in the 11th and 12th centuries in the Pyrenees foothills. Mont-Saint-Michel is a sublime example of a craggy eminence transformed into art: The rock of the mountain flows into the stone of the church. In ecclesiastical settings, just as stone is transformed by human art, so the divine dimension reaches down and transforms the human. When the unknown sculptor created the Smiling Angel for the cathedral of Rheims—sometimes said to be the first such expression in ecclesiastical decoration—he joined three realms of being, the mineral, the human, and the divine.

Perhaps, through distant atavism, I am drawn, superstitiously, as my Celtic ancestors were, to stones (as well as trees). Some attraction seems to adhere to stone; a bracelet of gems is far more to awaken in me little flickers of admiration and desire than is a gold necklace. I would not have supposed, however, that educated people today might believe literally in the power of minerals to achieve ends beyond those explained by physics. That is, until early in 2005, when I still lived in New Orleans. At the home of a friend, whom I'll call Lulu, I met a much younger woman—Elsa will do as a name. Her father had been on the Tulane faculty. She seemed lively and intelligent, but the fact that she had majored in anthropology might have suggested to me that she was interested in other belief systems. She had spent a few years in Mexico. Some weeks later, Lulu told me that she and I were both invited to Elsa's house, at 5:00, on a Thursday. Very nice. In New Orleans, a 5:00 invitation means cocktails and snacks or a buffet spread.

We drove uptown in Lulu's car. The house was a "shotgun" (a row of rooms one behind the other), near a commercial area where Tulane had purchased a site; plans for a high-rise building had been announced. When Lulu and I arrived and were ushered in, I noticed that the long main room, created when two or three walls had been knocked out, was empty except for very few pieces of furniture at the edges and some straight chairs toward the back. Elsa asked, "Would you like something to drink? All I have is water."

Stunned, but not speechless, I declined it. It's scarcely necessary to add that there was no food. Additional guests began to arrive. Two were kin in some manner to Elsa; I wondered how the others had been lassoed. I sat down in an isolated armchair toward the front of the room. After a brief while, Elsa came around with a tray on which small stones had been placed; I was told to choose one. "Curiouser and curiouser." I picked a yellow crystal the size of a walnut. She gave me a notepad and pencil and, showing her hand for the first time, told me to put in order of my preference five possible outcomes (of those she dictated) of the Tulane project. I made a show of starting to write but ceased as soon as she moved elsewhere.

Shortly, she asked us to move toward the straight chairs at the back, which she had set in a circle. There were too few, though, and some guests would have to sit on the floor. Lulu, who is stout, got a chair; she could not have gotten into a lotus position nor risen from it. I remained where I was. When pressed to join the circle, I said simply that I would rather observe. Am I a kindergarten child or trained animal to go into a ring? At first the chairs and participants were arranged in a single circle. Later, they were divided into two, concentric. Like me, the participants had stones, which they were told to warm in their hands; they were to think (not pray) that the proposed Tulane building would not, finally, be erected. Informational sheets were passed out (even I got one) about the extraordinary powers of divers minerals (moving mountains, influencing the planets); these powers were explicitly compared to the lesser ones, even the failures, of applied physics. (Indeed, human physical science has not yet moved planets, to my knowledge, though by means of rockets we would probably be able to set off its course a very large stone aimed at the earth.)

This ceremony endured for some while. I wondered what Lulu—not a stupid woman by any means—thought of it and how she could bear the hard seat. Participants recited phrases in unison, as I recall. Fervently, I wished myself away; had the yellow crystal really possessed powers, I would have been at home with a cocktail and some food. If I'd arrived by myself, I could have slipped out the door and driven away; but I had to wait for Lulu. Finally, following lengthy closing words, the rite was over. After we had replaced our magic stones, Lulu and I left quickly; she could move fast when she wanted to. Out of the rabbit hole, so to speak. When we'd stepped down from the porch and were out of earshot, she proposed that we go to a Mexican restaurant nearby. Once there, we each ordered a double martini, then large platters. Subsequently, the Tulane building project was canceled—not, I think, because of lithic powers, but because a few months later Katrina arrived, and the university found itself with $150 million of unplanned expenses and tremendous loss of revenue. Or did the stones work indirectly, by meteorological agency? Be careful what you ask for, we are told.

I return here to what I love—smooth boulders, a bit lichen-marked and mossy, around Grandmother's cabin, and the great building blocks that created such monuments as the cathedral of Chartres, the Norman abbey of Jumièges, and Vézelay. These edifices are essentially of the same substances as smooth little stones of various colors that I bought years ago at the Salmon Ruins (Anasazi) in northwestern New Mexico. They have been rounded and polished by a tumbling device that uses water and grit, the way our character, as I suggested elsewhere, may be smoothed by rough contact with the points and edges of other characters, as well as by the flowing water of spirit. I display these modest pieces in a small wooden dish, along with an arrowhead and a quartz crystal saved from my childhood. I think too of immense geodes in the Houston Museum of Natural Science, an elliptical amethyst specimen in particular; we have a photo of my granddaughter, Clara, next to it, just barely taller. With variations in age, method of creation, chemical composition, and appearance, all these stones are as one, the heart of the world, yet (since they really do not last forever) vulnerable, like our human hearts. I recall that as Pat and I drove in the mountains, I wanted to run my hands over the rocks, even the distant palisades and cliffs, which, in the clear air, beckoned. They are the very texture of life, jagged in places, planed off in others, with splendid façades shining far ahead even as other rocks surround us, and behind us pile up the boulders, the scree of the past.

How the Historical Novel Has Changed! Or, Should One Read Hervey Allen or Anne Rice?

WHY SHOULD THE QUESTION POSED in the title be asked at all? Why might a discriminating reader today even think of picking up either Hervey Allen's massive bestseller of 1933, *Anthony Adverse*, or *The Feast of All Saints* (1979) by Anne Rice, a hugely popular contemporary author? (Both are still available through major booksellers.) A literary face-off here between the two historical novels, chosen out of scores of works that might invite adversarial (if not saintly) confrontation, is instructive. They are not without resemblances—an illegitimate hero, questions of race and status (including slavery), and a New Orleans setting for Rice's novel and part of *Anthony Adverse*. Each illustrates the genre differently.

Allen (1889-1949), from Pittsburgh, graduated (according to the *Columbia Encyclopedia*) from the university there, then fought in the Great War. *Toward the Flame: A Memoir of World War I* records his experiences. He taught English in Charleston, South Carolina, and collaborated with DuBose Heyward on a poetry collection, *Carolina Chansons* (1922). He is best known for his biography of Edgar Allan Poe, *Israfel* (1926). According to 1933 interviews in New York newspapers, he spent five years composing *Anthony Adverse*. He later published other verse and fiction.

Anthony Adverse (1,220 pages) has broad chronological and geographical scope; the plot is elaborate, the characters numerous. For proper understanding and appreciation, readers need some acquaintance with art, architecture, languages, politics, and history (for instance, the early Napoleonic period). To be sure, this is a strength, not a weakness. Gruesome deeds are wrought. While those who devoured Dan Brown's *The Da Vinci Code* might be attracted initially by Allen's work, they would soon find it different—characterized by thoughtfulness and moral sensitivity, and without appeal to sensationalist tastes.

The term *picaresque novel*, used in reviews, is inappropriate. *Anthony Adverse* is not just a string of episodes involving a clever rascally hero who must live by his wits. Although Anthony, a man of his time, trades in slaves around 1800, he is concerned with morality and generally conducts himself honorably. Nor are other characters cardboard figures who simply advance the plot. Napoleon, convincingly portrayed, plays a not-inconsiderable role.

The writing is often poetic (no minimalism or Hemingwayesque spareness here), the vocabulary rich, the syntax good. A few errors can be overlooked. Exotic settings add their strangeness to chronological distance, but they are not exploited excessively. Natural features are described well, and human relationships with nature explored, notably when Anthony is a boy and, much later, when he lives by himself in the American wilderness, then is captured by Indians. The dominant metaphor is that of the tree, so like man in its birth from darkness, vertical growth, flourishing, and inevitable end. Despite violence, good taste is not assaulted. If you don't know what that means, don't ask; I won't tell.

In addition to its concern with justice, which Rice's novel shares, *Anthony Adverse* asks numerous other "great questions." How can a man understand himself without knowing where he came from? Human beings want to know that; blood does make a difference. Though the reader is informed of the facts, Anthony, an orphan, never learns his parents' identity or even nationality. (In this respect he is worse off than Rice's Marcel Sainte-Marie, a quadroon, who knows his mulatto mother and white father.) How should one respond to evil (particularly, the malevolence displayed by Anthony's mother's husband, who goes so far as to condemn him to near-certain death in a leprosarium)? How should one deal, in a class society, with one's inferiors? How can one live a Christian life, short of following Brother François, who returns good for evil and is crucified by primitive African fanatics? How can a man redeem his errors? What is genuine love of woman? Are intimations of spiritual reality mere illusions?

Rice is a manufacturer of bestsellers. Born in New Orleans in 1941, she was called, after her father, Howard Allen O'Brien; her mother found that "interesting." The child adopted the name Anne. Her mother died of alcoholism in 1955. Anne attended Catholic schools in New Orleans until the family moved to Richardson, Texas. Her husband of four decades, the late Stan Rice, a visual artist and poet, was a high-school classmate there. They went to California; Anne ultimately got a master's degree in creative writing from San Francisco State, where Stan taught that subject. In 1989, they left California for New Orleans. Her first novel, *Interview With a Vampire*, appeared in 1973. Subsequent titles, including such words as *vampire*, *witches*, *devil*, *damned*, and *mummy*, suggest exploitation of public credulity and ghoulishness. Her books have sold more than 100 million copies; Wikipedia calls her one of the most widely read authors of modern times. Three motion pictures were drawn from her work, and a 2001 miniseries was based on *The Feast of All Saints*. She herself wrote the text of a vampire musical, starring Elton John. In 1998 she returned to her childhood Catholicism. Two years later she announced her second departure, not just from Rome but from all Christianity. Her denunciation of religion was done in the name of progressive politics. "I refuse to be anti-gay. I refuse to be anti-feminist. . . . I refuse to be anti-Democrat."

There is more. Under the pen names Anne Rampling and A.N. Roquelaure, Rice composed what one listing terms "classic erotica," including *Exit to Eden* (1985), now in paperback. One commentator described her pornography as "explicit sado-masochistic erotica." "Her characters' sexuality is fluid, often displaying homoerotic feelings." She said that she looked for bisexuality in her characters. Her son Christopher, also a novelist, is a homosexual. *The Feast of All Saints* depicts homoerotic relationships, but without details.

For some readers, a *prima facie* case against her work has been made. Should such personal and publishing facts really bear, however, on literary appreciation and judgment? Many fine authors have been shady, callous, or perverted—some even moral monsters. I've studied quite a few myself. Perhaps Allen had a skeleton or so in his closet. (Information on him is scant.) At some chronological remove, moral factors are usually discounted. But that may be because genuine literary merit, confirmed by generations and with its own moral dimension, offsets what is otherwise offensive; or else time has eroded our sense of the author's moral deformities. François Villon, a thief and assailant, is a case in point. Perhaps such indulgence in judgment, or "the condescension of posterity," is not justified. Or we realize that the author of risqué material wished not to encourage perversion but only to make money or *épater le bourgeois*, though that cannot be said of the Marquis de Sade. What about current writers, our contemporaries, sometimes our neighbors? (In New Orleans I lived next door to one of Rice's three Garden District houses.) Certainly I should not want to enrich and encourage present-day pornographers by buying obscene books, no matter what their fame or purported literary qualities. The Rice novel in question here and one other came into my hands by chance, *gratis.*

In the present case, there is little need to weigh failings on which *ad hominem* judgments would be made against high literary value; Rice's 570-page novel, while readable, with a generally plausible story, is mediocre. What would one expect, given her sales figures? Fiction that draws 100 million readers is unlikely to be fine writing. Common readers used to appreciate better fare. Robert Maudslay, a sheepman from Ozona, Texas, recorded in his diary the contents of the library in the two-room stone house he shared with his brother before the sheep market collapsed under Grover Cleveland: a complete Shakespeare, a complete set of Sir Walter Scott, and the *Illustrated London News* going back to 1840. The basic literary education that enabled many ordinary people to value good writing prevailed, broadly speaking, well into the 20th century, perhaps 1940 or 1950. Though, like Rice's, Allen's novel sold very widely—the *Encyclopedia Britannica* speaks of its "great impact on popular literature"—and was reprinted, it is closer kin to Scott's and Victor Hugo's than to hers, and attracted readers accordingly. By the 1960's and 70's—those misbegotten decades—an expanding but undiscriminating population, schooled in relativism and do-your-own-thing morality by popular journalists and so-called teachers in trashy English departments, and exposed too little to elevated tone and contents in literature, generally expected, and got, sloppy writing, superficial depictions, sensational plots, and otherwise worthless, if not offensive, subject matter, instead of high truth and high seriousness.

Rice does demonstrate basic skill in plotting, in a narrowly defined fictional framework. The narrative carries readers along; one wishes to know what happens, just as, say, following a news report on an (allegedly) abusive "boyfriend," we want to know whether he has been apprehended. But that's just curiosity; to arouse it and then fulfill it takes no genius. Rice's only notable achievement is to depict sympathetically the lives and difficulties of French-speaking Free People of Color in New Orleans in the 1840's. Unfortunately, she calls them *gens de couleur libre*, rather than *libres*—making the color, not the people, free. Ah well, what does one expect from her and from Simon & Schuster, also the publishers of historian Doris Kearns Goodwin, for whom accuracy (in terms of crediting sources) was once shown to be unimportant? The Free Blacks or Black Creoles, with roots in the 18th century, remain a significant element of the city today. They populate several neighborhoods, churches, and schools, including Xavier University; businessmen, noted poets, craftsmen, professional people, and, nowadays, numerous members of the political class come from this segment of the population. Using invented characters and minor historical figures, Rice recreates its peculiar situation before 1865. Free in some respects (they owned property, including slaves), often cultured, sending their sons to France for school, the Black Creoles nevertheless faced restrictions in dealings with whites and, in response, developed customs such as *plaçage*. Whether Rice's interest in them arose from true appreciation or rather a desire to milk the topic for exotic value, thumb her nose at white New Orleans society, or profit from current multicultural fashion is unclear. Questions of justice that arise suggest her sympathy with the class.

Rice's expository style (everyone has a style, even inept students) is lackluster, characterized by basic grammar and diction errors, comma splices, missing commas, sentence fragments, lack of parallelism, dangling phrases, and other improprieties in syntax. (No proper copyediting, obviously.) The portrayal of the French Quarter relies on local color details and terms such as *banquette* (sidewalk). Much of the depiction is hyperbolic, and emotions are conveyed without shading and subtlety. Though minor, a few puzzles in the exposition are annoying. There are pages that I'd consider soft porn (not that I pretend to authority in the matter, even with my grounding in French literature). Readers interested in Free Blacks might enjoy and profit more from George Washington Cable's *The Grandissismes* and *Old Creole Days*, and Lafcadio Hearn's *Creole Sketches.*

When the historical novel arose in the early 19th century, it appealed to readers' feelings and their thirst for the past—particularly the Middle Ages—and for flamboyant dramas in exotic settings. But it was intended to be truth-bearing also, even inspiring, as understanding of behavior and events, and ultimately judgment on them, arose from the recounting and shaping of fact and imaginative additions. Well into the 20th century, good historical novels by modern authors helped depict and interpret the past. Though the genre lost ground to "true novels," cheap romances, and "suburban" fiction (*à la* John Cheever and John Updike), fine examples, especially concerning the American South and West (Wallace Stegner's *Angle of Repose*, for instance), were still produced after 1950. Rice's *Feast* is not, however, one of them. Of course, in a dentist's office, you'd read almost anything, right? But choose *Anthony Adverse* for broad design, beautiful prose, multilayered truth, and astounding goodness.

Four Modes of Book Collecting

If I have the book collector's gene—the gene that produces what Nicholas A. Basbanes, in his book on bibliophiles, calls "a gentle madness"—I have it imperfectly, either in a feeble form or else offset partially by other codes. I think the latter guess is correct; my collector's drive and the opposing impulses are like genes for hair, which often produce a blend of tones. Like many auto-assessments, estimation of myself in this respect is made possible by comparison with others. Some, known to me by reputation, are celebrated connoisseurs of books, often also maniacal readers, who could agree with Logan Pearsall Smith: "People say that life is the thing, but I prefer reading." Those I shall depict here are not of great wealth or celebrity, but are still more methodical, more engaged than I. Yet in my way I can join their company.

i

The most dedicated book lovers I know are a British team whom I met in the 1990's. I first visited them during Lent. London was very cold that winter; we ate hot-cross buns and drank tea in front of a small gas fire. These people are booksellers, not just collectors. "Unfair," you'll say; "that doesn't count. Theirs is a business." True—but not only a business. It is a *living* in the sense of "source of income" but additionally in the old meaning used for parish appointments in the Established Church—that is, a standing, a residence, an income, but also *a way of life*. They work out of their large flat, acquiring their stock by various means, including visits to estate sales, and carrying on their trade by catalog. Thus, like other secondhand book dealers, they must first accumulate their wares in individual lots, rather than ordering from publishers. They specialize in the antiquarian trade. They have, between them, French, Italian, Latin, and Greek (one of the team also lectures in French at a University of London college); they have large selections in those languages as well as 18th-century English letters, a favorite field.

Their stock of goods has expanded so that it has taken over the flat as well as their lives, like the crowds of words and metaphors, going well beyond the initial pretext, that took over the early prose style of Proust—sometimes his later writing also (like the style of Ruskin, Thomas Carlyle, and other

Victorians in certain critical works and novels). Cartons and crates of books are stacked on the stairs (theirs is the top floor, and the staircase leading to their door is used by no one else), in the hallway, on the floor elsewhere; shelves line the walls of the sitting room and adjoining dining room, where one cannot dine, the table groaning with heavy tomes instead of food (we always ate out); there are piles on end tables and footstools, a few in the loo, and many in the back exit, intended for fire emergencies but almost obstructed. Probably the kitchen likewise contains boxes and shelves; I've never seen that part of the flat. The visitor steps cautiously, as if playing hopscotch. One even sits with care, since the sofa and chairs likewise sport volumes that seem to have migrated there, looking for comfort. The impression one receives is quite the opposite of that, say, in Bauman Rare Books in Manhattan, a beautifully arranged shop, where you have only to mention a title that interests you and an elfin clerk is ready with a ladder to get it, in a movement that reminds me by contrast of boys who dive for coins in the sea to please tourists. (True, I don't know what Bauman's warehouse might be like.)

Year after year, many of my friends' volumes are sold; new acquisitions arrive to take their place. Thus their collections shift, as in other shops and in university libraries overflowing with new arrivals even as older books are taken off-site to what I call a "book barn" or simply discarded. But this is their *home*, not a shop. I have wondered at the system of classification. It would appear not to exist, but titles must be arranged for the catalog, and there must be a method, mad or otherwise, by which books can be retrieved when an order comes in. Some volumes, however, do not find buyers, or must wait for years. While bibliophilia is still with us—Basbanes assures his readers that "the passion to possess books has never been more widespread"—collecting has changed, as both levels of literacy and the taste for excellent writing have declined. (When Henry Wadsworth Longfellow visited England and was received by Queen Victoria at Windsor Castle, she assured him that all her servants read his books.)

Thus, while a man may still be judged by his library (though in *The New Yorker* James Wood asserted otherwise), which affords of him a profile, if not a full-length portrait, the number of competent judges has probably fallen. Anthologies, sets, and comprehensive editions have lost popularity; paperbacks have taken over much of the trade; ordinary publishers care little about bindings and other features that indicate quality. Collecting, as opposed to accumulation, has become more and more the undertaking of a happy few—and a small number of dealers catering to the same select company—who appreciate and can afford rare books and expensive editions, or who view such as "investments," along with artwork. Thus, in my friends' flat, countless unsold volumes, some handsome, remain—foster children, so to speak, who have become a permanent part of the family. Perhaps adoption is even foreseen sometimes. Like the British antiquarian bookseller Colin Franklin, the team may occasionally put on the market works originally purchased for their personal libraries—insofar as the latter may be distinguished from sale stock.

The most extraordinary thing about this team is that one is totally blind. Among the volumes on the dining table are always open Braille editions of large format. During visits the man remains seated there, his fingers moving over the Braille letters even as he joins in the conversation. His memory is, to be sure, extraordinary, his knowledge of publishing and letters remarkable, his languages at his fingertips. (The expression was rarely so apt.) Still, he cannot read order forms nor survey at a glance the titles on shelves, nor deal with miscellaneous piles or boxes of new arrivals or the dusty offerings for sale in an old library. Even knowing the skills of the blind, one marvels at his sure navigation among the shoals of cartons and loose volumes. Yet he is a true bibliognost. He discusses book collecting, bibliography, and individual works with striking acumen. I have seen him draw from a shelf a fine quarto volume bound in honey-colored leather, caress it, open it, and speak about it as though the letters were printed in gold before him. He is truly the ideal book collector, or rather the collector of the ideal, the titles shining on the shelves of his mind.

ii

A SECOND COLLECTOR to whom I can compare myself, modestly, is my grandfather. I remember him very well, though not in the years before his retirement, which took place before my birth. A 19th-century man of learning, he acquired books regularly through mail-order dealers and bookstores in Denver. His library eventually comprised thousands of volumes. They were not valuable in true bibliophilic terms—he did not purchase them as an investment, nor to assemble a specialized library to be donated to an institution—but some appreciated considerably in value. As a father of six and a physician, surgeon, state chemist, author, and professor at dental and medical schools (one of his specialties was what is now termed *pain management*), he could not have enjoyed great leisure during his early and middle years of practice. Yet believing, with Francis Bacon, that "reading maketh a full man," he devoured books when he could, especially from the 1920's on (when my father, the last child, was grown). Abundant reading then and even more during retirement is indicated by flyleaves on which he wrote the dates at which the volumes were read. While Grandfather was still in practice, I was told, he walked once a week from his office, in a downtown building, to the best department store, Daniels & Fisher, which had (like other such stores) a large book section. "Good day, Dr. Hill," he would hear, and then he would go make his selections. He also bought a box of chocolates weekly. After he retired, he continued to take the streetcar downtown every weekday morning, wishing (I believe) to maintain, insofar as he could, the routine of a man, and to avoid being at home while the women did their housework. He would go to browse among the books here or there, then to Baur's, a candy store, or to the D&F sweets department.

In addition, he received catalogues, and his name was on the lists of publishers who sold subscriptions to series. Among these series is the *Bibelot*, a 20-volume anthology of poems and prose, which I own. Additional sets of his included *Half-Hours With the Best Authors*, *Stories by Foreign Authors*, and *Famous Autobiographies*. Grandfather was thus a collector of collections. I have also from him four boxes of miniature books, more than a score to a box, from the Little Leather Library, probably bought by subscription; they contain such reprinted works as *The Taming of the Shrew*. Other miniature books of his similarly delight me; among them are George Washington's *Rules of Behavior* and *The Physician's Interpreter*, for diagnostic purposes, in four languages. Grandfather retained the eclectic tastes and broad aspirations of the 19th century and thus, rather than "spot-collecting," bought widely: biographies, histories, volumes of art reproductions (far inferior to what is available now, but still worthwhile), books on plants, insects, geology, geography, exploration, and music. He bought poetry but not fiction, I believe, unless he had reason to suppose it was of unusual interest. One volume I was surprised, and pleased, to find among his things well after his death was a finely printed translation of *Les Chansons de Bilitis*, by Pierre Louÿs, a late-19th-century piece of artistic erotica.

Books were not forgotten on his travels. I have before me Volume 11, *Spanish Papers and Salmagundi*, from a set of Washington Irving's works published in 1868. The flyleaf bears, along with the date "5/22/46," the stamp of "Kauffman Curio Store, Navajo Indian Blankets, Rugs, Mexican Work, 312 Main Street, Grand Junction, Colo." When my grandparents visited Japan in 1938, he bought a volume on ikebana and bonsai, published that year, called *Selected Flower Arrangements of the Ohara School*. The text is in Japanese and English. The volume opens like an accordion, with all the pages connected, beginning at the right. (Since pine trees are featured along with flowers, leaves, bamboo, and fruit, it is fair to use the term *bonsai*.)

Grandfather gave me countless books when I was a child, purchased with me in mind, and mailed others when we moved to Texas; he also handed down to family members innumerable volumes he'd bought but did not choose to keep. While we were still in Denver and saw my grandparents regularly, almost every week a book or so would change hands. That is to say, Grandfather was a recycler; he knew how to get rid of some books while keeping others. Books represented mental more than material capital. What were his grounds for divesting himself of things? I do not think it was lack of space. He had his study, and shelves lined the wall in the basement; he had a small lab there also, with more bookcases. Uninspiring writing made a book not worth keeping, perhaps, or absence of new information. In some cases he viewed the work as ephemeral but knew that someone else would get use from it. "Pretty poor stuff," he had written on the flyleaf of a collection of poetry, which, I believe, was handed down to my father. Barely worth buying, barely worth reading, but perhaps of brief interest to someone else, in this case because my father taught English, and inferior writing can be useful as a measure of what is superior.

iii

The third standard of comparison for me is my husband, who cares for books immensely and has accumulated thousands. He rejects the term of *bibliophile*, with its connotations of wealth used to purchase rare editions, nor would *bibliolatry* be a good label. But there's a bit of bibliomania in him and more than a bit of the connoisseur, in general. He has professed never to have discarded a book when he was young—nor many since then (and few that were good, he assures me). When he gives away a work from his library, it is a second or third copy. Unlike me, he did not know a grandparent; his father had immigrated from Ireland, and though his mother was born in America, she was a late child and her Danish parents did not survive into his childhood. But a Danish aunt, with good judgment, gave him worthwhile literature during his boyhood—*Treasure Island* and *Tom Sawyer*, to start with. Thus did he learn to cherish books. He owns several editions of each of those classics, including translations, but the earliest volumes have pride of place. In 1958 he asked a friend who was in England to choose £100 worth of books for him at Foyle's, in Charing Cross Road. That was a large sum for the time and for his budget. Much later, in Portland, Oregon, he visited Powell's, the used-book store, which, he learned, had acquired much of Foyle's stock—*déjà vu, déjà lu* (we suppose), but not *déjà (re)vendu.* At some date he arranged with Kennys (*sic*) Bookshop in Galway to select and ship to him each year Irish books, costing up to £200. That arrangement continued for ten years or so.

To prepare for his move from his gentleman's ranch back to Houston in 2005, he hired a high-school student to pack one shelf of books per box.

Upon their arrival, he unpacked them—some 160—and, with a coded list, replaced them on their shelves, though not usually in the identical order. Thus large clusters in his collection remained together—Irving, Stevenson, Mark Twain, Faulkner, Charles Darwin, Richard Haliburton, Charles Lindbergh, other books by or on explorers, books on ships, Irish letters and history, songbooks, poetry. He has smaller clusters too, but otherwise there is not much rationality in the collection, which expanded for years while he did not have time to keep it in order and perforce overflowed case after case. He asks me sometimes to find for him a particular volume. "What color is the binding? How big is the book?" Sometimes he knows, on other occasions not; but he is always right in thinking it is *somewhere* in one of his 29 bookcases, which occupy most of the wall space. His mental inventory is thus good, the shelving less so.

He must constantly confront the problem of new books. Each year he spends hundreds or thousands of dollars on orders from the numerous dealers who solicit his custom. He records in a notebook the date of purchase and the price; in a second list, he notes the year when they were read. Like my grandfather, he does not buy much fiction, though a series of Pulitzer Prize winners found their way into his library, some good, some less so. He cares particularly about dust jackets and preserves them well. He is fond of luxury editions—boxed, large format, fine bindings with gold lettering, handsome title pages and endpapers, good printing, wide margins. Illustrations delight him. Where are the oversized luxury books to be kept? Right now, like my bibliophile friends in London, he has quite a few on the floor. He nearly always reads these expensive volumes, whereas his shelves (like mine and many others') hold numerous other books unread for one reason or another. Some years ago he acquired from the Folio Society a nine-volume edition of Pepys's *Diary*, supplemented by an *Index* and a thick *Companion*. He read every single word, including the footnotes. Finding an error in one note, he informed the publisher of it. In return he received a message of thanks, in which it was remarked that no one else had identified the mistake. Might we suppose why that was so?

iv

This brings me to myself, a more erratic collector. Now, I am, in important ways, my grandfather's intellectual descendant. Of his six grandchildren, three led professional careers, John as a physician, Edward as an archivist with the National Archives in Washington, and I as a French scholar and professor as well as author. Perhaps I am the closest to Grandfather. I have been served by much longer life than these cousins. I have been also more engaged in scholarship and writing that continued after retirement, just as Grandfather studied, took notes, and collected specimens well into old age. I am not, however, such a book-buyer—more a *rat de bibliothèque*. For nearly 40 years, I had within a few feet of my library carrel at Tulane large holdings of French literature and literary criticism, sections of which I had helped assemble and knew so well that they could be viewed as "my" collection. I could step out, turn a corner, and pull from the stacks the work I wanted to consult. In some volumes I left scraps of paper with useful page numbers and brief notes for future use. Using pencil, I corrected misprints and factual mistakes. Meanwhile, publishers sent me books for review and textbooks for classroom adoption, and my shelves at home and in the office sagged with periodicals.

Nonetheless, I did purchase books, of course, especially in France and England, during summer visits, in New York when I went there frequently in the 1960's, and in the French bookshop in New Orleans that a former student of mine ran, successfully, for some while. Writer friends contributed many works to my library. My books are not kept with my husband's but in a separate location—a flat in the same building—which serves as my office. One shelf is filled with the admired (and expensive) Pléiade editions, most with scholarly apparatus, of major French authors; similarly well-bound and well-designed French reprints in other series occupy another shelf; art books stand at the top; and so on. I have hundreds of French paper-bound books, mostly from Gallimard, the preeminent French literary publisher for a hundred years. Many of these, printed in the 1950's, when French book manufacturers still used cheap paper, as before the war, are in such bad condition that the spines are illegible, if not missing, the covers are torn or lost, pages have fallen out, and the paper has yellowed, nay, turned brown and, in some cases, brittle.

Why do I keep them? In fact, in connection with my move to Houston in 2007 I took armsful to the trash bin. And just now I have put quite a few others in a recycling box (not passing them on for reading, as Grandfather did, but for paper pulp). Many remain, however. The chief reason for holding on to stuff that, otherwise, is good mostly for such pulp is that the editions are the first in which I studied the respective works. Valéry's poems are better printed by far in the Pléiade edition and have notes (the editors', my own), but I initially encountered them in this discolored paperback, almost falling apart now. To reread them there, with my early glosses on difficult words and, among other marginalia, Professor M.'s remarks summarized, is to return briefly to student years, to see again through the wondering eyes of the uninitiated. How else can I read *Charmes* again for the first time? In my bookcases there are still dozens of such cheap books, particularly by poets, but also Proust, Gide, Camus, and others. If, as I wrote above, I made myself discard some just now, it is not by a healthy reaction against sentimentality, nor because shelf space is dear (though it is). The awful fact is that, on darkened paper, my handwriting of yore, much in pencil and of necessity small, has become illegible to my well-used eyes. Though I am presently at work on a lengthy paper concerning Gide, for which it would behoove me to re-examine marginalia of the past, it would be impossible to make out any gems in the old editions; so they, like the grass, are gone. Might an employee emptying the recycling box retrieve them? Unlikely; more's the pity.

To cast out these old book friends took resolution; but it was, I confess, liberating; it freed bookcase space and allowed me to let go of something. And here is where I rejoin the very author whose works I have just thrown away. For Gide himself knew about liberation from belongings. "One thinks one possesses, but one is possessed," observes a character in *L'Immoraliste.* In the course of his career, Gide tried out various sorts of moral and intellectual cleansings, starting with his first trip to Algeria, when, attempting to rid himself of the millstone of Calvinism, he deliberately left at home his Bible (asking later, however, that his mother send it—a typical Gidean about-face). He preached, and occasionally practiced, a kind of vagabondage that required what he called *dénuement*—deprivation, or stripping; one must travel light, metaphorically and actually. (At other times, a perpetual lover of contraries—he was both stingy and generous—he shipped with him during his travels several trunks, with books and personal items. One may note in this behavioral syndrome both Christian asceticism and the capitalist impulse of accumulation as attributed by Max Weber to Protestant cultures.)

In 1925, some while before he left on an 11-month journey to Africa, Gide sold many of his vast library holdings. Doing so brought him cash, for among books deaccessioned were valuable ones, some having become so because they were early, usually autographed, editions of works by authors since grown famous. Doing so likewise brought, doubtless, the satisfaction of freeing himself from them, from the bondage they seemed to constitute, and setting out on his journey untrammeled. Chiefly, he was delighted to part with presentation copies floridly inscribed to him in the past by erstwhile friends who in the meantime had, privately or publicly, denounced him as a perverter of youth. He was, but chiefly of those who wished to be corrupted; and the accusers, notably Claudel, were not all angels.

Years later Gide was asked whether he did not regret abandoning volumes dedicated to him by Claudel and Francis Jammes, for instance. He replied, "It is less indecent to get rid of books that one no longer cares about than to make a place for them in one's house. Does one continue to receive friends with whom understanding has become impossible?" Another friend from the past subsequently sent him a book bearing the dedication, "To André Gide, for his next sale."

Not partaking of Gide's notoriety, I have no such valuable library holdings to winnow out and no such impulse. Nor do I acquire many new volumes now; my husband does that. "Collecting," however, need not mean just "adding more" or buying valuable books for pleasure, through thirst for possession, or to insure the future; it implies also caring (in both senses) for one's collection—curating it. I do so. I know where most items are, notwithstanding the lack of a catalogue. Sturdy spines are generally well aligned. Grandfather's books and those inherited directly from my parents or my aunts—some of which had passed through Grandfather's hands first—are well treated and shelved nicely, after their peregrinations. Small lamps above the shelves illuminate them. It does not bother me that three volumes which my parents had rebound after years of use (John Bartlett's *Familiar Quotations*, G.M. Trevelyan's *History of England*, and *A Miscellany of American Poetry*) stand out as rather homely because the titles were written by hand in white ink by the amateur bibliopegist. The Pléiade volumes—some so used in teaching and research that they, like the paperbacks, are worn—are close by. My nearly complete holdings of works by Jules Roy, a novelist (a bibliophile also), and Jean-Claude Renard, a poet, deeply religious, if idiosyncratically so, stand together. A Steuben glass bowl and two French engravings add art to a shelf. My numerous holdings in American poetry are clustered together, as are runs of quarterlies, including *The Sewanee Review*. Of the cheap editions and other books in bad condition, many are on lower shelves, partly screened by the piano, so that their shabbiness escapes visitors' eyes; others are in a back hallway. Apart from these concessions to appearance, everything is for use, not for show, in contrast to the handsome sets, purchased for clients by interior decorators, that are all binding and nothing else.

Six new books, sent by their authors, arrived by mail in the last week. Whether worth my time or not, I'll keep them for the moment. Perhaps they, or others—including treasures formerly mislaid and forgotten, recently rediscovered—will lead me today to say, with Eugene Field, "Let my temptation be a book."

Along the Bayou

Bray's Bayou is an important natural waterway in Houston; two others are White Oak Bayou and Buffalo Bayou, which in its easterly portion becomes the Houston Ship Channel, 50 miles away from the Gulf of Mexico. We see Bray's from our windows. Houstonians, like many Cajuns, pronounce the last syllable of *bayou* as an *o*, but of course for me the word retains its proper Louisiana, and French, pronunciation. Bray's, which is not a sluggish waterway, is fed from natural sources upstream, other bayous and ditches in the city, and drainage conduits under the streets. Flowing in an easterly direction, Bray's cuts through neighborhoods in the southwest, south, and east and debouches into the Ship Channel. It is a pity that the sole "parade of boats" I know of here is downtown on Buffalo Bayou and not on Bray's, where thousands of people whose homes are in the vicinity could admire the vessels from its banks.

Bray's belongs to the city, and along most of its urban course on both sides lies grassy parkland, often wide, like fairways, with walkways and bike paths. In our immediate vicinity, it runs along the southern edge of Hermann Park, paralleled by a roadway on the left bank (as one faces downstream); its right bank marks the edge of the city land. Our high-rise property is immediately adjacent to it. Thus it is "our bayou," and its birds are "our birds." Young trees near the roadway are almost "our trees," since they are tended by volunteers from the building. Perhaps in the past the city sold off this plot of land and others nearby—like a museum deaccessioning paintings worth many millions in order to raise cash. (Since this is done frequently by institutions small and large, don't mislead yourself by thinking that the Courbet or Monet you've donated will stay there necessarily.)

Years ago the channel of Bray's Bayou was lined with cement, covering the channel and high embankments, but, with residential development, flooding became endemic in the southwest area through which it flowed. During the great storm named Allison, in 2001 (before I moved to Houston), the water came onto this property, thence into the lower garage, two basements of the building, and lobby. That's millions of dollars in damage. (Far more was done in many important buildings elsewhere.) Much of Bray's and its verges has now been redesigned and extended in a major civil-engineering project to raise its banks and widen the distance between them, thus providing bigger overflow space. I have never seen the bayou dry; even in the drought of summer 2011 the current was strong, and I could espy fish of ten inches or so in its depths. Despite these recent improvements, the water can rise very high. In winter 2012 three heavy rains brought it well above the banks and over large areas of grass and construction sites nearby, making it as wide as the Seine. Similarly, in May 2015 there was tremendous flooding right under our windows, and a foolish man, wanting to investigate the inundated areas, went out in a canoe and was drowned in the strong current. At least three new residents in our building moved here subsequently, having lost houses on streets that had not flooded previously during their residence. After nearly 40 years in New Orleans and thus exposure to frequent floods, including Katrina, which I lived through, I visualize such inundation easily, too easily; any prospect of flooding is unsettling.

Yet I find great contentment in gazing down at, driving past, and walking along this bayou, which remains, despite engineering, a natural feature, with an unexpected presence and interest in this great urban complex. This pleasure derives partly from its curves. The curve is nature's most pleasing line. The naturally snaking course of the waterway has been preserved. In our immediate vicinity, it makes two turns at nearly right angles, and there are intermediate sinuosities. Major roads follow the bayou; others cross it on its numerous bridges. Farther west, Braeswood Boulevard (the spelling suggesting, misleadingly, lovely Scottish scenes) runs sometimes on one side only, elsewhere on both, with the traffic divided by direction. Near us, Holcombe Boulevard crosses the bayou, and Braeswood intersects with Holcombe there; then, renamed Macgregor Drive, it runs almost parallel to it for some distance. A few yards from our garage there is an iron footbridge; a new one downstream, over-engineered but of very pleasing design, with fine arches, is wide enough for motor traffic but limited to bikers and pedestrians. A vehicular traffic bridge, combining utility and beauty, opened upstream just yards away a few years ago; its emplacement, handsome sentinels, and beautiful lighting remind me of certain Paris bridges. This bridge carries the traffic of Cambridge Avenue from Holcombe across the bayou to Macgregor, then enters Hermann Park, curves around the zoo, and ends across from the Rice University campus.

Readers should not be discouraged by these details. The point here is not to test their ability to reconstruct the picture but to give a sense of urban design, with curves, roadways, and bridges organized around a natural bayou. The interesting shapes produced thereby include an irregular triangle, which contains the Ronald McDonald House and the Houston Hospice, across Cambridge to the west. This is all in the midst of the Texas

Medical Center, a complex of hospitals, several medical, dental, and nursing schools, research centers, specialized treatment centers for cancer sufferers and others, offices, three major hotels (with others on the periphery), and parking garages, furnishing some 73,000 jobs (we are told). It's one of three city centers in Houston. (The others are Downtown and the Galleria district.) Night and day, the traffic flows back and forth; night and day, fire engines and ambulances scream and flash their lights (Patric calls the latter "meat wagons"—his sense of humor is Irish); medevac helicopters buzz across the sky, reflecting the daytime sun by their yellow or red paint, lighting the darkness like fireflies. And night and day the bayou runs, affording us some of the pleasures that make lives worth living and saving. With the park (its golf course surrounded by woods) to our north, the Veterans' Hospital campus to the south, and a Catholic property to the east, with a chapel, convent, and home for the elderly and infirm, all landscaped with live oaks, cypress, pines, and other local trees, and the stream flowing by, we are almost in a glade. It is pleasing to think that many ill and feeble people can look from their windows onto trees and running water.

Surely my taste for bodies of water, from small ponds to the ocean, was nurtured when I was a girl in Colorado—by what I saw and what I could not see. While one can admire fine mountain streams there and even rivers or what bears that name, the state is not defined by water. (Like those of Wyoming, the boundaries are straight lines, and large seas are inconceivable.) Any mountain stream, any tarn were delights to me; I liked Cherry Creek, which ran through the city quite near our neighborhood, and could follow it on various walks. Even when I was young, I knew, through my parents' talk about reservoirs, the value of water, so much scarcer now and more expensive in many areas because of foolish use and huge population expansion, as well as severe droughts in California and elsewhere. The rarity of water was even more obvious in West Texas than in Colorado. Such experience is instructive. In 1996 I visited friends in Catalonia who lived 25 miles from the nearest town of size. It's a dry land, and their water supply was not ample. So they asked me to try to use water sparingly. At the end of the week, they commended me on my thrift—extraordinary, they thought, for an American. I explained that my girlhood had been spent in the arid west.

During my three years at the University of Florida, I became well acquainted with the shores and waves on both coasts. Numerous poems in my first collection, *Watering*, came out of time spent at the beach and in the surf. I could imagine the waves as great, majestic seahorses pulling behind them the huge chariot of the surf. Numerous ocean voyages have revived that sense of the water's incantatory power. But streams and rivers are just as appealing, perhaps more so in some ways. The ocean, as we experience it, is whole and stable; though waves lap at the shore continuously and tides rise and fall, such great bodies of water do not flow, whereas, as writers from Heraclitus till the present have observed, streams run on, an image of our lives. Their fresh water responds to thirst or even awakens it; their liquid is crucial to our bodies. In it, we are baptized; and, like Elijah, who crossed eastward over the great river of Palestine, the Jordan—a symbolic crossing into salvation—we imagine crossing the deep waters of the unknown into a new life. There, we hope, in the words of Robert Lowry's hymn, dating from the Great Awakening, to "gather at the river / that flows by the throne of God"—as if the Lord Himself loved a stream. Though Bray's Bayou, far from the holy lands and their vision of paradise, is an urban stream, and its cement verges do not have the attraction of a natural overhanging bank covered with grass or moss and large trees bending over the water, it flows, it's usually clear, it carries my thoughts.

Readers of my poetry know my affection for birds, from cardinals, gulls, and others to large waders. As though they had been designed for the purpose, birds are the image of a powerful human aspiration. Icarus was not wrong to dream; his technical arrangement failed him. Air travel is gratifying in a way, for its speed and (sometimes) convenience, and planes and vapor trails can be lovely against the blue or gold of skies. But no sight of a plane, no travel above the clouds can compare with the glimpse of a hawk soaring above the trees, or a blue heron taking wing, or a great egret flying slowly just above the water. The difference comes, I believe, from the visceral feeling of rising and planing inspired by birds. Through imagination, we almost sense in our bodies the movement of flight; as the bird's wings beat, I picture my arms flailing in the air, I sense the currents around me, I soar. Such transport becomes, easily enough, a sense of spiritual elevation. Birds are the inhabitants of the ether, the airy image of spirit.

In and around the bayou this year there have been the usual great egrets, herons, hawks, ducks that we identify as "American black ducks," even a pelican. The ducks and egrets sometimes visit the pond on our property; its goldfish make a good meal. We also have had whistling ducks and Wilson's phalaropes—a mated pair, we believe—and now there is a "mystery bird," a fine flyer, with a large wingspread, pointed wing tips, and a white underbody. Patric observes: "He has a lot of fun. Who wouldn't have a good time with a pair of wings like that?" Our bird books, authoritative and comprehensive as they wish to be, did not allow us to identify that bird with certainty; later an ornithologist confirmed that, as we suspected, it was an osprey. Cattle egrets often score the blue; they nest in the park, I believe, like the water birds and hawks, and they occasionally visit the verges of the bayou. In the morning

I sometimes see at the edge of the water small flocks of birds that resemble sandpipers. Their plumage appears iridescent, and they walk as if on tiptoe. In the trees on our property there are songbirds: cardinals, mockingbirds, and birds in blue plumage that aren't jays; they often feed on the bayou parklands. Ordinary urban birds are around, too—pigeons, finches, sparrows, grackles, crows, and an enormous number of swifts. Many of these collect on wires in large gatherings; others peck around the hedges and grass. With rabbits, turtles (large ones in the bayou, smaller in our pond), and fish (the variety unknown to me), this is almost a wildlife preserve.

As these pages suggest, Houston, often maligned, has attractions, as well as being a livable place (lots of residential high-rises, reducing sprawl; and the traffic grid is well laid out, and movement along the thoroughfares not too bad most of the time). True, while the park is wooded, the bayou embankments are not, nor are they planted with azaleas or other fine shrubs. Moreover, after the drought of 2011, numerous trees in the park, mostly live oaks, and on the Veteran's Hospital campus died. Others, especially cypresses, are still alive but look very scruffy in the cooler months. Alas, many trees right near us were felled last year to create additional parking spaces. (Oh, the Druid spirits must be very angry.) One source of pleasure, whether I am outside or in, is that of space, restful to the eye and the mind. I don't need much space in my rooms; what counts is what I can see.

I also like walking outdoors. This walking is for pleasure and exercise. I should prefer that it fulfill an additional function—getting me to a shop or the post office or a bank branch. That is the ideal: beauty and utility in one. But the layout around here is such that in the immediate vicinity there is not much variety in the commercial establishments; apart from medical buildings, most are hotels, eateries, and banks. So I "go out for a walk," trying to move along fast. Unfortunately, long years in New Orleans made me wary of parks and nature walks, perhaps too shaded. My outdoor exercise there was mostly by way of errands along well-traveled streets in the Garden District. A woman, it's true, could go for exercise to Audubon Park in the daytime in good weather and be confident that numerous other walkers, runners, and bikers, some from Tulane and Loyola, across the avenue, would be on the track that goes around from St. Charles to Magazine Street and loops back. The Audubon golf course is in that area also—but golfers are so preoccupied that I'm not sure they would pay attention to a scream. But I said the *daytime*; early morning and dusk were not safe, and nighttime should have been ruled out. But girls and women went anyhow, and some were attacked. Some also walked on the levee at night or went out in parks elsewhere that have paths, but are less frequented, and I recall hearing of awful assaults, with rape always and usually murder also.

While Houston isn't the cradle of crime that New Orleans was and, to judge from reports, remains, still, I am circumspect; I go out only during hours when others are around, preferably on weekends, when the foot traffic is considerable. It's a favorite track for dog-walkers, runners, cyclists, along with young parents pushing baby carts. Many come from this building, which has well over 200 condominium units and lots of dogs. Others must come from the few single-family residences nearby, the townhouses on Cambridge, two high-rise condominium buildings on the north side of the park (and a new one under construction immediately adjacent to us), and other townhouses and apartment buildings within sight—and offices and labs at lunch and after work. I can monitor the comings and goings as I sit at my desk and ascertain, according to the traffic, whether I want to go out. There is a choice of pathways. If Patric accompanies me, we walk slowly; then he stops at the east side of our garage and sits on a bench until, having sped around, I loop back.

Though confined, like the destiny of everyone else, by verges and channeling—that is, the facticity of the past and our present circumstances and situation—and now visually confined by the new building next door, an oversized eyesore that blocks out the sunset, the course of our lives runs well. Patric and I have enormous advantages, countless blessings. We are essentially free, in all the rich significance of that term. Sartre suggested once that, to judge by the way God created the human race, He must love freedom more than goodness; since they may be incompatible, depending upon the use or misuse of our liberty, human beings were given the greater gift. (Sartre did not believe in God but was capable of imagining and writing about Him.) We wish to use this freedom well.

Every day flows into the following days; every bridge leads to something or someone. I'd like to follow the bayou downstream in a canoe or a gondola, letting friends pick me up in their car a few miles away. Since that's not done here and I'm certainly not the person to inaugurate the custom, we'll just watch the water, cross bridges together, observe the birds, and sail on imaginary wings or currents of thought.

In Defence of Poesie

MY TITLE, borrowed from Sir Philip Sidney, is deliberately misleading; that is, it does not mean here what he intended when he used it for his work, published posthumously in 1595, known in another edition as *The Apologie for Poetrie.* In the past, poetry needed no defense—if that word means pleas to a hostile or indifferent audience. Sidney, a member, along with Edmund Spenser, of an important poets' club, was also a royal appointee and a soldier, who, as a volunteer, received a fatal wound in an attack on the Spanish fleet for the relief of Zutphen, in the Netherlands. His influential treatise offered an examination of poetry in his time and considerations on the essence and principles of the art, especially in relation to philosophy and history. His contemporary Sir Walter Ralegh was likewise a military man and explorer as well as a poet. To know, appreciate, perhaps write poetry was, for many, part of the gentleman's role; and it was entirely compatible with vigorous action and manliness. In the final act of Ben Jonson's play *Poetaster: or, The Arraignment* (1601), Augustus Caesar rises to his feet in acknowledgment of Virgil's entry and seats him in a chair more elevated than his own. What was "defended" in treatises and certain poems and plays was the distinctiveness of poetry, its aims, means, effects, and appeal. Advice, both general and particular, was offered; models were proposed, and aesthetic principles set out. Even Socrates, in the *Republic*, and Aristotle spoke in defense of the art.

The high standing of poets endured for three more centuries after Sidney. Dryden and Pope were honored, the latter even a "celebrity." With the advent of Romanticism, poets aspired to be viewed as prophets and seers. Writing in the 1790's, Mary Wollstonecraft called poetry "the first effervescence of the imagination, and the forerunner of civilization." In his tract "A Defence of Poetry" (1821), Percy Bysshe Shelley asserted that poets were "the unacknowledged legislators of the world." It should be noted that this hyperbolic remark was a reply to Thomas Love Peacock's rather sarcastic claim, in "The Four Ages of Poetry" (1820), that during the "Age of Iron" or bardic age—the period before civilization—poets were "not only historians but theologians, moralists, and legislators." For Peacock, that is, poetry was a surviving feature of a primitive world. Shelley understood the matter differently. Nineteenth-century poets enjoyed great popularity. Tennyson was madly admired, even mobbed. It will be recalled that, during a visit to England in 1868, Longfellow was assured by Queen Victoria, in an audience at Windsor Castle, that all her servants read his books.

In France poets similarly had enormous prestige from the Renaissance on, into the 20th century. Voltaire was admired throughout Europe for his verse. The Romantic poet Lamartine, who, as readers will remember, boasted to a detractor that his book would soon be in every cobbler's pocket, was what is now called an activist. After a short diplomatic career, he was elected to the Chamber, wrote a history of the Girondins (1789 Revolutionaries), and was the people's idol during the Revolution of 1848. Victor Hugo, who was in his time recognized foremost as a poet (as his sales figures showed), not as a novelist or dramatist, played a political role in 1848 before going into exile in 1851 in protest against Louis-Napoleon, and, from the Channel Islands, continued to criticize the Second Empire. He remained beloved after his return to France. People scrambled to get his books of verse. Hundreds of thousands of admirers filed under his window in 1881 in an organized celebration to honor his 80th year, and a million mourners, it is said, lined the route taken by his hearse four years later. Vigny, though politically and socially conservative, depicted the poet as seer, yet foresaw that in the industrial world poetry would lose prestige. The hero of his play *Chatterton* (1835) is obliged to justify the role of poetry in a society based on utilitarian principles. (When challenged, he answers that the poet is the one "who reads in the stars the route shown to us by God's finger.")

At least until the Great War audiences for poetry in France, England, and America remained large. Julian Bell recalled that, at Cambridge in the late 1920's still, "the central subject of ordinary intelligent conversation was poetry." By the later 20th century, however, the practice of poetry had been turned on its head. Reviewing an anthology called *Postmodern American Poetry*, the late Alaskan writer John Haines lamented the "loss of the public voice" and "the shift in writing from substance to technique"; contemporary poetry as represented there seemed to him generally "cut off from normal discourse and apparently content to speak to itself alone." The pleasures and importance of poetry have been so discounted that innumerable adults look upon it as an alien undertaking. As Kevin Gardner wrote in *The Sewanee Review* in 2015, "Lovers of poetry are no doubt an endangered population, particularly in the U.S., where poetry may be esteemed, yet has little popular regard."

Poets themselves—literary and often social radicals—have been partly to blame, along with editors, critics, particularly the postmodernists, and teachers, who incorporated into the curriculum the worst critical trends. Radical critics turned on those with cultivated taste and discernment. Form and formality were taken for priggishness and moral tyranny. That has gone on for decades. It is fashionable to attack the contemporary "canon poem," one that refers to earlier models in form, treatment, and tone, and having, presumably, older cultural assumptions. Why pay obeisance to offensive antediluvian motifs and traditions—classist, sexist, racist?

Rumors about the death of poetry in the Occident are, to be sure, exaggerated. To judge by various indicators, Americans, in great numbers, love poetry, or what is taken for it. An extensive, prominent industry is based around it. In raw terms, large numbers of people have connections to it, and like it, or claim to. Taxes—federal, state, and local—support it. Innumerable organizations and foundations do likewise, using their own funds and government grants. Lectures, conferences, readings, workshops, open-mike sessions and "slams" in coffee shops and bars, prizes and awards, publications of many sorts, specialty bookshops, online sites, radio readings, presidential-inauguration poems, National Poetry Month (April), poets-in-residence in schools and colleges—all indicate how, since the 1960's, poetry has become a major cultural player.

Poets' prestige is recognized in high places; Robert Frost read at President Kennedy's inauguration, and—showing the steep decline of standards in slightly more than 30 years—the pseudopoet Maya Angelou at Clinton's. Almost all the states, plus many counties, cities, and the nation, have a poet laureate. Billy Collins, a former U.S. and New York laureate, said, "The country is crawling with them. I think it's out of control." Some national laureates (formerly "Poetry Consultants to the Library of Congress") were very good and deservedly eminent: Allen Tate, Robert Penn Warren, William Carlos Williams, Frost, Richard Wilbur. Saint-John Perse (the diplomat Alexis Saint-Leger Leger), who in the 1940's held a privately funded position as a quasiconsultant, won the 1960 Nobel Prize for Literature. (As secretary general of the French foreign ministry, he had been obliged to flee Paris in 1940.) The Russian-Jewish émigré Joseph Brodsky, poet laureate in 1991, was another Nobel Prize winner. Recent state laureates include accomplished, nationally respected figures such as Kelly Cherry of Virginia and David Mason, who held the Colorado laureateship for a four-year term. Some make admirable efforts for their state: Mason visited all 64 Colorado counties, and Darrell Bourque of Louisiana, another poet of achievement, was similarly enterprising. In contrast, the forgettable first poet laureate of Houston, Gwendolyn Zepeda, had not yet published a collection of verse when she was appointed in 2013; she had in print only stories, with a tasteless title, and a novel identified as "chick lit." In 2014 the North Carolina appointee resigned after a furor over her credentials, two self-published books. (Governor Pat McCrory attacked the critics' "hostility and condescension.") However the public reacts to such appointments, the term *poet laureate* in newspapers does attract attention.

Yet despite its apparent popularity, to service-industry and blue-collar workers, tradesmen, even most college students and white-collar professionals, poetry probably is alien. Even in *The New Yorker* (which publishes some hundred poems annually, few very good), how many subscribers read the verse? Note that, in addition to poets, of which the present writer is one, the organizers and administrators of poetry programs, teachers, purveyors of materials, participants, and their families are not disinterested parties. How many rival organizations and their members receive their attention? How many books of poetry do they borrow from libraries or buy each year? What are your chances of finding good contemporary poetry in your local high-volume bookstore? People will spend hundreds or thousands of dollars for tickets to musical and theatrical performances, go to gallery and museum openings, and collect expensive coffee-table books; but buying a volume of verse would not occur to them.

Nonetheless, the output of verse is huge. Certain monthly magazines and major quarterlies continue to run poems in every issue, and countless "little" magazines publish verse. Innumerable new poetry collections and anthologies appear every year, with imprints ranging from Norton and Knopf through university presses—Illinois, LSU, Wesleyan, Yale, Chicago, Mercer, Georgia, and others—to independent presses, some known only locally and among aficionados. Some newspapers still review these books, and some people (as well as libraries) must buy them—just not those I mentioned above.

Then there is the Association of Writers & Writing Programs, "the world's largest network of literary patronage," composed of nearly 50,000 individual and institutional members. Known by its original acronym, AWP, it was founded in 1967 to promote creative writing in post-secondary English departments. The campaign was successful. There are presently some 500 such academic writing programs, many of which grant advanced degrees. They turn out hundreds of graduates, who are likely to become teachers in similar programs. AWP underwrites 125 writers' conferences and centers and itself puts on the largest literary conference in North America. Not all members are poets, of course, nor all the programs devoted to their art; fiction and, increasingly, creative nonfiction are popular fields of study. Yet poetry is often favored, being easier to compose (no plot line to manage) and get published piecemeal, and often more accessible. Curricula may include, as at NYU and the University of Rochester, literary translation at the bachelor's and master's level. There is a market for poetry translations; Malvern's Books in Austin, for instance, displays a wide selection of French, Spanish, and Russian poets, including new versions of works already available.

Poetry occupies a place also in primary and secondary schools. It is thought to be within the reach of all—truly a democratic medium. The very schools that turned away from traditional verse and its appreciation (including memorization) and from its moral content and presumed elitism spend enormous sums on "poets-in-the-schools" and many class hours on creative writing. In addition to regular classroom instruction, there are readings and workshops offered by visiting poets. Diane Raptosh, Idaho's writer-in-residence, gave one, it is said, on a school bus. The blogger Elena Aguilar, a "transformational leadership coach" from Oakland, California, explains why poetry should be taught in schools: It helps build a sense of community; it allows "kids" to express sides of themselves or experiences they might conceal otherwise—hurts, family discord. (Thus it is therapeutic.) It gives opportunities for speaking and listening; its rhythms are appealing; and it suits those with inferior English because in poetry rules may be broken; students may use foreign words or even compose in a foreign language (but can they really write it?). Thus, for the 150th-anniversary celebration of Boise, Raptosh, then city laureate, read poems using local slang, Spanish, and Somali. For the "sense of community" aim, consider the campaign organized by Juan Felipe Herrera, a former California laureate and, as of summer 2015, poet laureate of the United States, directed toward having pupils use poetry to "shape their feelings about bullying into collective expression." A British poet, Fiona Sampson, wisely argued, however, that "poetry is not a tool for teaching other things." Not primarily, that is, in its essence.

Further evidence of enthusiasm for poetry comes from prisons. Prisoners are, to be sure, a specialized population, living under restrictions and often in need of diversion and counseling. Numerous poets listed in the online directory of Poets & Writers (a large New York outfit) indicate their willingness to make prison appearances. Richard Shelton visited Arizona facilities for decades, after an inmate on death row asked for comments on his writing; work by Shelton's students has been published. In Nevada, a poet holds workshops in a nearby prison several times a year. There are podcasts and handbooks for prisoners and programs featuring their products. Although the aim may be reform, such activities serve initially as outlets and therapy. One cannot gainsay wholesome prison activities, of course. Doubtless, however, the standards are low.

The popularity of poetry in schools and prisons springs doubtless from its facility and generic malleability. (Just say it!) It is not only democratic but also open-ended and serviceable for political and social indoctrination. Liberals, who largely dominate educational organizations and institutions, apparently believe it is appropriate, indeed their duty, to impress their views on captive audiences, where there is little likelihood of objection. The prominence of many widely published poets is due to their public embracing of righteous causes. Sharon Olds, for example, a winner of major prizes and now on the lecture circuit, has focused on global injustices as well as sex, child abuse, and violence.

Much of what passes for poetry is, in fact, bad, some very bad, some offensive. (Olds's writing, for instance.) Free verse predominates, seldom appealing to the ear; in many quarters it is the only form. The late Miller Williams, who read at Clinton's second inauguration, composed a poem every morning, he said. Of course not all were published; the writing may have been mostly exercise, or therapy. But if a poem can be dashed off, without further thought, why not? The easier is ordinarily more appealing than the challenging, whether it be one's livelihood or literary expression, or both. There is a lot of trash, and you wouldn't want certain poets around your children. Coarse realism—an unspeakable vulgarity—is a cachet of sophistication and achievement. At a public library where half a dozen teachers and graduate students from the University of Houston presented their work, little was good, poetically, and much was coarse. Here is an example of annoying verse, probably extemporaneous, showing skill in condensation and juxtaposition, but otherwise valueless. It is titled "At the California Institute of Technology." The author, Richard Brautigan, associated with the counterculture movement in San Francisco, was poet-in-residence at that institution in the winter of 1967. Following, or perhaps leading, other institutions, the Cal Tech authorities must have supposed that poetry would exercise a humane influence on its engineers, chemists, and physicists.

> I don't care how God-damn smart
> these guys are: I'm bored.
>
> It's been raining like hell all day long
> and there's nothing to do.

This is the entire poem, widely available on the internet. The people of California—or someone—paid for this fellow to be on campus. What a waste.

As this example suggests, self-indulgence (poetic, psychological) is rampant; the poet's ego is thrust in our face; artistic discipline and self-control have given way to indolent writing that, as David Orr puts it in his *Beautiful & Pointless: A Guide to Modern Poetry*, consists in "Here I sit, having poetic thoughts." The effect is infantilism—like children's or lunatics' efforts. The "thoughts" are generally *feelings*, trite (hasn't everyone been happy or unhappy?), vague, or hostile. America being a society of *feeling* more than of reasoning and reflection, such writing pleases many. As Valéry remarked, however, feelings do not make good verse; by themselves they are incapable of creating a single good line. "To *feel* does not mean necessarily to *make felt*, and still less, *beautifully felt*." The view remains valid. In a 2016 interview with Judith Pulman, Mason remarked, "Mere raw expression of one's personal pain is not art." Even worse are tantrums, or what John Wain called "the ravings of a drug addict." (For an illustration of recent years, see the poetry of one Brenda Shaughnessy.)

Verbal beauty, viewed as snobbish and elitist—to be feared like the plague—though once within the ken of nearly everyone, has been thrown overboard. Ears are no longer attuned to sound values; regular forms, which often lead poets to their best lines, have been abandoned. (They are based on *rules*, widely unpopular now, of whatever sort.) From the Romantic period until the mid-20th century, at least, lyric poems from many languages, by Goethe, Heinrich Heine, Victor Hugo, Tennyson, and Paul Verlaine, for instance, as well as verses by Shakespeare, were set to music, usually lovely melodies, by serious composers; subsequent poetry tends to irregularity and does not lend itself to melody.

Instead, brief evocations, images for the eye dominate. Painterly descriptions are generally disdained, however; strange juxtapositions, surprise, incongruity, shock—modernist poetic values inherited from the early 20th century—are exploited excessively. An additional unfortunate characteristic is an arrogant, willful obscurity, another modernist legacy. The results are pretentious.

What Americans accept most readily in the way of verse is common rhymed or metered lines such as those in greeting cards (which sell by the millions), rock music, rap. Another important vein, doggerel, must not be overlooked. Smutty verse circulates underground or in trade and professional circles; cowboy poetry festivals attract thousands of devotees. Limericks without number are collected and appreciated by many. Even traditional Christian hymnology has been replaced in certain circles by inferior songs with guitar accompaniment and, sometimes, gestures.

To defend poetry to a general audience, then, is to risk confronting readers' skepticism and misapprehensions. The genre is notoriously difficult to define and discuss anyhow. Terms such as *content*, *form*, *style*, *image*, *symbol*, and *metaphor* cannot be pinned down; aesthetic categories such as the sublime lend themselves even more to disagreement. Why talk about poetry at all? From the observations above, it would seem there is not much left today of good quality. Though the composer John Cage suggested that, while nothing was accomplished by listening to a piece of music, "our ears are now in excellent condition," we must recognize that American ears for poetry are not in good condition. When the much-lamented Michael Jackson is labeled an artist, how can we identify and honor good verse of the past and present? Well, one might pay attention to poetry simply as an antidote to Jackson (like playing selections from Johann Sebastian Bach loudly on your car radio when vile noise emanates from a subwoofer in the next lane) and in defiance of others who have contributed to degraded taste. We owe that to ourselves.

How will such attention pay off? Poetry offers knowledge, experience, morality, verbal beauty, and order. Those 20th-century critics who suggested that form was everything went too far; matter counts also. "Art and matter in poetry are perfectly distinguishable . . . neither is of any value without the other," observed a wise commentator. Unlike the back and front of a lamp, which is an entity but which, given that some is hidden, the brain must reassemble as such, these interconnected aspects can and must be viewed together. In varying proportions, they constitute a whole, not a sum of discrete parts. Whereas *some* knowledge and experience are often available in bad as well as good poetry, morality, beauty, and order are largely confined to writing of the past and a minority of poets today.

What knowledge is worthwhile is another matter. No discourse on the topic can be fitted in here, but it is scarcely needed, since common sense can generally serve as a guide. Knowledge may be conveyed explicitly (episodes of the Trojan War in the *Iliad*) and may be factual; or it may be indirect, subtle, or a blend of fact and imagination (Evangeline as imagined by Longfellow); it may be mostly speculation (how one can think about plums). Such knowledge may be old or new. To write poetry, asserted Willa Cather, is "to say the oldest thing in the world as though it had never been said before." Yet, as Dylan Thomas observed, in *Quite Early One Morning*, there is such a thing as new understanding. "A good poem helps to change the shape and significance of the universe, helps to extend everyone's knowledge of himself and the world around him."

Experience (even "feelings") may be the poets' own, that of others, or, ideally, experience of the poem itself. Speaking of poetry as *connaissance* (knowledge), Claudel argued that it was also *co-naissance* (co-birth). To know something of value or know it anew is a type of creation, a renewal. While European poetry always included a subjective element (pleasing personal lyrics on nature in the Middle Ages, dense poems on erotic love and religious devotion in the Renaissance), the role of personal experience became much more prominent under Romanticism ("the overflow of powerful feelings," in Wordsworth's term). Subjectivity has dominated poetry since, despite modernist and postmodernist experimentation; formlessness favors subjectivity. The 1950's confessional school and its innumerable imitators produced the excesses of ego and self-dramatizing referred to above. Poetry workshops in the schools feature little else. The question is whether this experience can and should be communicated to others, and, in Valéry's word, beautifully. Somehow, the poem must evoke in readers' sensibilities an experience of value or provide the pleasures of recognition—the experience being "ne'er so well expressed."

Morality would seem to be a *topic* of poetry, not an aspect of it. Much canonic work is now dismissed because of its moral messages, its preachiness. This is so notwithstanding the subtlety and delicacy with which many earlier poems treated moral issues. But today's right-thinking poets (antisexist, antiracist, anticolonialist, and so on) do not mind beating *their* drums in verse. Without much skill, certainly without genius, they end up with work much less inspired than that of the canonic moralists. As Eudora Welty wrote, with modern letters in mind, "The zeal to reform, which quite properly inspires the editorial, has never done [literature] much good."

The best narrative and dramatic poetry of the past embodied moral excellence by its own characteristics—what Matthew Arnold called high truth and high seriousness. Evil was duly identified and punished; poems praising depravity and wickedness did not achieve greatness. Even scurrilous verses that vilified enemies and erotic or scabrous poems, unfit for the young, generally aimed at some sort of truth or beauty. "To please and instruct"—that was the goal of poetry according to Horace in his *Ars poetica*, echoed by Boileau and Samuel Johnson. For poetry to accomplish these aims the poet must have moral convictions, and there must be consensus among readers on standards of behavior and beliefs. Alas, that is why it is not frequently conceded today that poetry can be moral; if there are no standards, if every code, even moral anarchy, is valid, then the very idea of moral excellence is false. (But *diversity*, as currently understood, can be promoted, of course.)

These three aspects—knowledge, experience, morality—are, in a good poem, in harmony with its words and their arrangement, that is, its beauty and order. Poetic order illustrates and helps satisfy the need for personal and universal order; ordinary language likewise does this, but poetry goes further, being *an order within an order*. Words disposed according to established rules or even the subtler arrangements of good free verse (with shaping, beat, sound echoes, and aesthetic discretion) are inherently pleasing to the Occidental mind, ear, and eye. Rhythm, appealing sound, repetitions and variations satisfy by themselves and as evidence of the hand and mind at work on the world's material. Numerous observers, Claudel among them, have pointed to the connection between the stresses of poetry (various sorts of long-and-short or strong-and-weak sound patterns) and the human heartbeat, with its systolic and diastolic rhythm. (In prosody, or verse analysis, the term *diastole* is applied to the lengthening of a short quantity or syllable.)

The principles of verse are not identical in the different modern Occidental languages, but all have patterns of one sort or another, and rhyme is found widely. Conventional French verse used a syllabic count, chiefly in 12-syllable lines; English favored the iambic foot (unstressed-stressed), mainly in pentameters. Free verse of varying types has been effective since the late 1800's in France, where, since versification did not depend on fixed beats, poets were accustomed to using other resources, easily retained and cultivated in free verse. Claudel favored what he called *versets*—long free-verse lines based on biblical verses. Apollinaire often used rhyme and octosyllabic lines, though he eliminated punctuation. Saint-John Perse, Francis Ponge, René Char, Pierre Jean Jouve (a tormented Catholic poet), and my late friend Jean-Claude Renard cultivated very short, incisive prose poems.

These examples and others that could be drawn from the body of French poetry from 75 to 100 years ago—long enough for winnowing to have occurred—show that those poets who have risen, and stayed, above the sea of 20th-century mediocrity overcame the drawback of license, even randomness and nihilism, proposed by the extreme avant-garde of their time, particularly Surrealism. Their writing achieved a type of classical expression, whether drawing on the ideals of concision and precision, long honored in France, or on other sources (the Bible for Claudel).

It is encouraging, in a way, that among those knowledgeable enough to have any opinion at all, even modest, on current poetry, one would find widespread disillusion. The common reader retains some sense of what a poem should and should not be. Art—style and form—is expected. Cather wrote, "There is nothing so unmistakable as a true poem." Before rapping, before the screaming and gyrating of Jackson and similar performers, popular songs furnished models of meter and rhyme, at least; country music remains influential, though western declined. Good poetry is still not unknown in a few schools. Other models come from the Christian hymn tradition. An abyss lies between Brautigan's product and verses by George Herbert, John Milton, and Charles Wesley—and translations from the Greek *Didache*, Latin chants, and 16th- and 17th-century German hymns.

The general picture is unlikely to change, since the progressive current dominates American culture and will do so increasingly, as illegal and legal immigration allows millions of foreigners, many with alien traditions, to settle in the United States and exercise social and political influence—whence the popularity of writing by and for the unlettered and unassimilated. In the foreseeable future, there will be, increasingly, low standards, vulgarity, and ignorance. Whether highly trained or simply attuned to older poetry modes, those who can recognize and value canonic verse and that of today's best poets will probably decrease in number, and better writing will decline in value, according to Gresham's Law. It would be useless and wasteful, however, to try increasing its appeal by making it worse. Good taste, fine skills, and what David R. Slavitt calls "the morality of vision" do not easily allow of adulteration without losing their essence. What is well imagined, well crafted, with attention to every aspect of poetic art, cannot become more useful by being transformed into popular idiom.

Useful, I have written. Poetry must not, however, be viewed as utilitarian or, it was stressed, a tool. Yet *non-utilitarian* does not mean without place, without purpose. Poetry appeals to our senses and emotions, stirring us, soothing us, sending us soaring. Perhaps it is also like love: hard to define, not strictly necessary for physical existence, but fundamental to our natures and to all we deem worthwhile. You can scarcely live without it. We must rely on ourselves and our fellows, not the common millions and their Pied Pipers, but small circles of readers and writers (including, we hope, converts)—those intellectual and spiritual kin who appreciate poetic value. The pleasure of a well-wrought poem is the fulfillment of its aspects. It is broadly cultural; at its finest, it is vision. It deserves and needs a cultivated and supportive audience. While language by definition has meaning, poetry provides heightened meaning. The poem is where valences change.

Adventures With Food: Or, The Ideal Meal

Every November, *The New Yorker* turns over one of its issues to writers on food and their supporters, the food-industry advertisers. (Why do I continue to read that magazine, which I have criticized in print, notably in this very book? Since Patric subscribes in order to read the book reviews and enjoy, or attempt to puzzle out, the cartoons, every issue is close at hand. It's part of what "one reads." Leafing through, week after week, I know to avoid various rubrics, contributors, and topics—tasteless, trashy, socially offensive, or simply of no interest to me—but certain articles are worthwhile.)

Now, these food writers, and the audience to which their pieces are addressed, may be true gourmets—that is, connoisseurs of fine eating and drinking as we understand it, mostly on the basis of French models from Jean-Anthelme Brillat-Savarin forward. But I believe *The New Yorker* writers on this topic and, I think, their readers, can be classed generally under the rubric of "foodies," a term introduced by Paul Levy and Ann Barr and popularized in their 1984 volume, *The Official Foodie Handbook.* "Foodies" are those who love food for consumption but also for study and "food news"; they watch the food shows on television, patronize farmers' markets, and spend money at fancy culinary-product stores. They may favor and wish to promote, for gastronomic or cultural purposes, exotic foodstuffs. They often boast to their friends about their cooking triumphs or visits to the top-ranked restaurants of their city or distant places. They are the ones to whom are directed flashy newspaper sections on edibles, recipes, and restaurants, such as a piece in this week's paper announcing that "Uchi [a Japanese chef] brings sexy back to the table." There are even "foodie movies," I read, such as Gabriel Axel's *Babette's Feast* and Fatih Akin's *Soul Kitchen.*

In the food issue, I first browse, looking at the ads touting champagne and gourmet tourism, for instance, directed to what a journalist calls "gastronauts." Then, in the book announcements, I note titles such as *New American Table* and *1,000 Vegan Recipes.* Then I return to the table of contents. Numerous pages are devoted each year to what their authors view, apparently, and wish us to view, as *adventures* with food. Restaurants and purveyors of edibles, such as fishmongers and cheese shops, are described, their owners profiled, the chefs praised as gastronomical geniuses; varieties of ethnic foods, some genuine, some recently concocted takeoffs, receive extensive and laudatory treatment. Capitals of gastronomy are surveyed, not so much Paris and other traditional seats of culinary excellence in France (too well known already, in fact, and too mainstream) as new centers—Tijuana, Los Angeles, and Quebec, for example (though I see that Eataly is a prestigious destination for gastronauts). There are recipes or what can pass for them. "Secret ingredients" are given out by professional food writers and well-known figures such as the author Paul Theroux. "Celebrity foods" receive attention in the magazine (as in newspapers). Personal experiences with food and especially Thanksgiving dinners, as provider or consumer, are recounted (for instance, how an American woman tried to prepare a traditional Thanksgiving feast in Morocco). Old aunts and odd dinner guests get to appear in these sketches. The historical dimensions of nutrition and eating customs are not neglected, as a review of Henry VIII's menus shows, nor the scientific ones (how food is colored, shipped, and stored, the health value and chemistry of various products, the making of different wines). Rather unsavory details (unsavory to me, at least) are sometimes included.

The whole array of offerings is unappetizing because it is hyperbolic, not necessarily in its language (though there's a good deal of campy style) but in its suppositions. The face-value assumption is that there's something wrong with you and your circle if you do not already know the names of certain trendy foodstuffs and ingredients. (I think of the fruit called açaí, all the rage recently.) Numerous words unfamiliar to me are not glossed; the dictionary does not suffice because many are foreign. Behind this attitude is the more fundamental implication that, if not already a convert to stylish eating, you should become so—you should be saved. You ought to study at the feet of the food writers and abandon your own ways. It's all bait: Read our pages, and you will learn what sophisticated, cosmopolitan dining is; patronize the restaurants we tout, buy products made glamorous in our ads, go on gastronomical tours to California or more exotic lands, try the unusual offerings of street vendors, as described in our pages.

Of course, this magazine, albeit read by thousands of subscribers elsewhere, is directed initially to New Yorkers (certain types, at least), then to those who wish to be, would like to emulate them, or believe at least (and not without some basis in fact) that Manhattanites are the arbiters of taste. I do not. (Readers of this collection are already familiar with certain opinions of mine connected to that matter.) In other words, food is treated in its pages like literature and the theater—something on which, when it comes to good judgment, New York is assumed to be the acme of enlightenment, the avant-garde. This is an aspect of what Stephen Miller, writing in *The Sewanee Review*, called "Manhattanism," an undefined but recognized culture that acts like a magnet.

This recent widespread food-faddishness, both symptom and cause, is almost a cult. Food, I thought, was basically for nourishment of the body. True, in the long process of civilizing himself man transformed the primitive consumption of food—first by introducing food to fire, next by refining the preparation of ingredients and enlarging the range of natural products known to be good or tasty, then by acknowledging the dimension of social intercourse in the act of eating and ritualizing it. The feast is an ancient and formal expression of hunger joined to that other need, for fellowship. With Plato, we have a banquet; in Christianity, which carried further (on other models) the mystical dimension of a meal, we have the Eucharist or Lord's Supper. Significant events—weddings, baptisms, coming-of-age rites, funerals, signing of contractual agreements, launching of ventures, and countless other moments in our collective life—are marked by sharing a meal, as were many such events in the distant past. Food is not merely a way of staying alive.

Thus, I am not against refinement in such matters—on the contrary. I am for civilization rather than barbarity. The poet William Alexander Percy (whose poem "They cast their nets in Galilee . . . ," set to music, is in the 1940 Episcopal hymnal) wrote that "manners are essential and are essentially morals." Manners are, in fact, more important to me than the offerings on the table (if one assumes some plausible Western standard of preparation, dishes, and table usage). Manners include correct and proper speech, as it prevailed in my parents' and grandparents' houses, and its tasteful use. Would I rather be served an ordinary meal in a pleasant ambiance at a table well set with silverware, china, a linen cloth and napkins, or at least cotton, attractive wine glasses, and good, cultured company—or partake of gourmet food cooked by Chef So-and-So in unattractive surroundings (noise, for instance), and with boors as companions? The alternatives are not often so stark; the grounds for choice remain.

Nor am I against attractive presentation of food, nor attentive service from waiters. (Such niceties can be maintained at home, by the way.) But there is something obscene in turning food, for which we should rightly give thanks, into a fetish, an object of worship. This nation is awash in food, not just because of its resources and industry but because, by today's ethos, abundance, indeed a surfeit, must be displayed—surfeit of restaurants, courses per meal, varieties, the servings piled high on platters at the angle of repose. "Sufficient" doesn't suffice. The public responds accordingly—by turning eating into a cult practice and by overconsuming. On various cruises Patric and I have taken, we saw passengers rush by the scores to the counters of the self-serve restaurant, attack the platters, and take back to their tables plates that should have satisfied two, if not three. Food was available from 6:30

AM to 11:30 at night—from continental breakfast in the morning through hot breakfast and luncheon to ice cream in the afternoon, then dinner, and late-night treats. To judge by their girth, many travelers had spent hours at such buffets. The sort of gluttony I denounce is not identical to food snobbery—more to the contrary, it would appear, since *nouvelle cuisine* (not so new, presently) and the far-fetched combinations thought up in fancy restaurants in America are generally on the light side, compared with Shoney's and the Golden Corral, truly a pig-out establishment. (We stopped in one in Topeka, Kansas, driven by hunger and the traffic patterns. Never again.) Food snobbery and gluttony do have in common, however, an exaggerated attention paid to menus and dishes.

My complaint is not that we neglect the Starving Armenians (of my childhood), the Starving Sudanese and so on (of today). This essay is not about collective guilt or distributing foreign aid. We cannot by any means turn over to those in need elsewhere the surplus we have at any meal or in any grocery store; food would rot, and its equivalent in funds would be friable, turning to crumbs in various pockets and rarely arriving at its destination, as reports indicate. (Look at the results of aid efforts after the Haiti earthquake.) Moreover, these other peoples do not like or refuse to eat much of what we might have to offer; and their rulers (one can scarcely speak of "governments") often exploit donations for their own benefit and in such a way that the destitute are even worse off than before.

It's not even a question here of the so-called "epidemic" of obesity that infects this nation and, by now, much of Western Europe. (It has become, as it were, endemic.) To be sure, I am outraged by the figure of $850 million or so in the federal health budget for anti-obesity programs compared with the $350 million to be spent on Alzheimer's research. Unlike that degenerative brain disease, the cause of which is unclear and the remedy for which has not been discovered, we know what causes obesity in almost every instance; pathological cases make up a minute percentage, and as a true malfunction of the body must be approached differently anyhow. As my dear friend Evelyn, a diabetic (and never overweight), noted, the ordinary solution to corpulence is simple: "Eat less."

The principal matter is, in my mind, one of mores, even of morals. Gluttony was among the seven deadly sins. In general, excess is to be avoided, and that includes excessive refinement. If extremes have value—and I believe they may—it's because, circling around, they touch, complementing each other; we, at their meeting point, become the middle term. Perhaps we need them, philosophically speaking. But not in ordinary life. Moderation is where we belong. What *The New Yorker* food issues and innumerable gourmet magazines promote is essentially a sybaritic culture. It fits and reflects the narcissistic, self-indulgent ethos of this age. In 1975, Craig Claiborne enjoyed a $4,000 meal in Paris, the result of a winning bid at an auction. He and his companion stayed at the table for five hours and ordered innumerable dishes but ate very little of each.

There have been, of course, fashions in various human artifacts for as long as we know—in hair, headgear, clothing, tattoos, in carriages, furniture, cars, and countless other practical objects and bodily adornment, as well as the fine arts. Though they are shaped in part by materials at hand, fashions are constituted by varied, often imaginative utilization of these materials—going beyond their raw presentation—as well as available techniques and tools. Thus we are familiar with gastronomic fashions in previous centuries, often springing from the valuation of rarity, as the wealthy enjoyed (presumably) not only the expensive foodstuff or beverage (such as coffee) but also the presence of it in their lives as a sign of prosperity and proof that they were acquainted with the new. The cult of novelty in the Western world currently is so enormous, so ingrained, that ordinary supermarket products, for instance, are regularly repackaged and renamed—sometimes really modified a bit—so that they can be labeled "New." The presence everywhere of novelty, or what passes for it, and the craze with which it is cultivated do not signify its value. What's trendy may, or may not, be better. The current craze for unpasteurized milk, especially in California, leads people to pay $10 for a gallon of what I get for $3 or so. This rage, like various other food fads, certain trends in healthcare—therapies and self-help—and extreme positions taken by some in the ecological movement, is part of a wider development I shall call romantic primitivism, a phenomenon more than 200 years old, which runs now underground, now on the surface, overflowing sometimes, nearly taking over.

I am, you see, a snob—an anti-food-snob snob. What is wrong, I ask, with ordinary cooking? Eating, said (mostly by advertisers, it's true) to be an art, is not like art at all. Nor is drinking. A 2012 show at the Smart Museum in Chicago called "Feast: Radical Hospitality in Contemporary Art" featured among its "participatory projects" an event, repeated on a number of evenings, titled "The Act of Drinking Beer With Friends Is the Highest Form of Art." (This is what one writer, Chris Ritchie, called a "democratic experience," in which "everyone has an input into the progress of the show.") In art one seeks what is superior, since that is its *raison d'être*; by their very aspirations the fine arts (as distinguished from crafts and practical arts) constitute a transcendence of the common that appeals to the mind and spirit. Sound becomes music, speech becomes poetry, rough stone becomes a cathedral;

and vision, whether that of a landscape, garden, person, or the interior vision of the imagination, is expressed and transformed in painting. The implications of food journalism notwithstanding, food does not go beyond itself; its appeal to taste and sight is decorative, not essential. (That edibles, like other natural objects, may have metaphysical suggestions, I do not deny. More on that below.) To listen to the finest musical creations, and to visit Notre-Dame de Paris, mean going beyond the self. Shivers, sometimes physical as well as mental, accompany such experiences; they are the touchstone. While a fine dinner, particularly with friends, can be a delight, as it attracts the senses, nourishes our bodies, and may offer the occasion for enlightening conversation, it is not transcendence; food is one of our earthiest markers, the very substance and condition of our embodiment.

Thus a robust meal of roast beef, potatoes, a green vegetable, *au jus* gravy, almost translucent, as my grandmother prepared it, is wholly as deserving of gourmets' praise as menus proposed by the food writers. Fried chicken used to be good, before Colonel Sanders and his corporation made its name synonymous with junk food. It is not suitable for banquets, to be sure. (Emily Post replied to a reader asking how one should eat a drumstick at a dinner party, "Fried chicken is not to be served at dinner parties.") It fits nicely on the menu of a family gathering, a picnic, a civic celebration, for which, as for formal dinners, there is a set of appropriate, if informal, manners.

Something almost sinister enters the picture here. It is the disdain of influential figures, and many who have absorbed their prejudices, for basic American culture (in the anthropological sense of the term)—that is, for what was developed in the colonies, chiefly on English, Scots-Irish, and German foundations, and spread, with modifications, throughout the states and territories in the 18th and 19th centuries, prevailing through the early 20th century, until after 1950. I think of my mother's cornbread, my Canadian grandmother's meat loaf and pound cake, the smoked ham my Aunt Margaret liked so much. Along with disparagement of such foods, including New England boiled dinners, farm cooking anywhere, Southern cooking from Virginia to the Deep South, Texas dishes ("Tex-Mex" is pejorative; everything Texan is disparaged by the "elites"), and other "country" foods such as corn on the cob, the disdain I mention is fundamentally directed at descendants of those who first produced it and lived by it—landowners, farmers, ranchers, merchants, their employees, city laborers, and others. Only cooking traditions connected to the formerly marginalized are excepted from general blame. Thus the plain folk dishes of Louisiana (red beans and rice, jambalaya, gumbo, crawfish) have some standing. Soul food is fine, too, as long as you don't assimilate it to Southern cooking in general. Multiculturalism has hit the world of eating, as well as everywhere else. "Fusion" is the thing. There's antinationalism, too. If the dish you consume in the United States is foreign—hummus, for example—that's even better, since, in certain circles, foreign trumps American, as we know, in diet, mores, and, I fear, religion. In a geodesic dome in Hawaii, serving as a test and experiment station in connection with future exploration to Mars, the crew, from the United States and Canada, had for their dinners such treats as pho, sushi, and falafel along with gumbo and ravioli. (The last choice is surprising.)

Now, some readers of my poetry may observe, wryly or even with a vein of sarcasm, that it is strange of me to criticize snob food and foodies. First, did I not live in New Orleans for nearly 40 years and thus dine from time to time at Antoine's, Galatoire's, Arnaud's, Gautreaux's, Commander's Palace, Clancy's, and so on? Yes, over the years, though Antoine's is overrated. Elsewhere in Louisiana I had the joy of dining at Café Vermilionville in Lafayette, Morel's in New Roads, and Mervin's in Houma, all appealing by history, architecture, greenery, and setting (Mervin's on the Intracoastal Canal, with barges passing by, and Morel's on False River, an oxbow lake). But remember that, wherever we are, most of us live normal lives, taking care of families and attending to business and profession. Such dining out was exceptional, not routine; it's tourists who eat night after night at the big-name establishments. What's more important, the restaurants I've named all feature one cuisine—Louisiana Creole, based on standard French, with variants. Experimentation is unusual in such kitchens; one expects and gets the traditional dishes. Gastronomy is cultivated, certainly, but without radical touches. In short, the restaurants serve gourmet meals, not foodie fare.

Am I not, though (people suppose), a Francophile? And doesn't it follow that I am a connoisseur of upscale restaurants in the French mode, some of which may be experimental? Haven't I indulged in overrefined dinners in the crucible of gastronomy, the home of the greatest chefs and still an inspiration to food writers? (Adam Gopnik's 2011 book is called *The Table Comes First: France, Family, and the Meaning of Food.*) Well, not really. True, my devotion to French literature is deep, as to certain other Gallic achievements and features. That doesn't make me the sort of Francophile that you meet at French clubs; still less does it mean that I ate often at famous restaurants in France. My reactions often parallel Gide's: "Famous restaurants make me flee." Twice I was a guest at celebrated French establishments—one, Lasserre, in Paris, the other, L'Espérance, in Burgundy. The latter meal was in the company of Jules Roy, his wife, and a small circle of his friends. The ambiance was cordial, the evening delightful. The owner-chef, Marc Meneau, visited our table. So I did my best to show my appreciation. It took effort, however, for the dishes were rich and some were unfamiliar, though still Gallic, of course. I like to recognize what I eat—the basic ingredients and the preparation. A 19th-century French writer quotes an epicure as saying to his cook, "If I know what I eat, I'll dismiss you." For me, no mystery dishes, thank you, still less exotic dishes from halfway around the world. That rules out restaurant surprises.

Ah ha! That must mean I have no palate, no appreciation of fine food, and am not venturesome—thus I should be disqualified from addressing the topic. Nevertheless, might I have a better palate than readers will suppose? When Kate, my daughter, was young, she and I kept a list, like the AP Top Ten in football, of the worst meals we'd had together. (As for memories of *good* meals, you may test me on those also.) After she went off to college at Chicago and then was in graduate school at Columbia, we spent less time together and shared fewer meals; now, as a wife and mother, she has her own tastes and kitchen. I daresay, though, that she remembers at least three of those awful dinners, one a Tunisian creation, another centered on a "liver pie," the third—well, I have almost obliterated it from recollection. But I can recall the occasion—a visit to a family in Florida. The hostess had recently gotten poison ivy on her person; when we arrived for dinner and an overnight stay, she undid her belt and rolled down her clothing a bit to show the red blotches. Using that discomfort as an excuse, she declined to prepare the dinner and instead lay on a couch like an odalisque and directed her husband in the kitchen. He probably did his best to carry out her orders; but the result, if memory serves, was a tasteless, watery *ragoût*, almost inedible. Many years later, Kate was not with me (fortunately) when New York friends prepared for me another candidate for the top ten, of which the centerpiece was an Oriental fondue, featuring some strange product (not bread) for dipping into peanut oil. I should have said I was allergic to peanuts; I am too honest. The whole meal was revolting and nearly gagged me.

Nor do I like to cook. Another disqualification! An acquaintance asked me how, given that dislike, Patric and I managed—did we eat out every evening? But I didn't say that I *didn't* cook, just that I wasn't fond of it. From age 17 on, most of my dinners have been prepared by me; even when I was 16, I cooked hot lunches for my father five days a week, since my mother taught some 30 miles away. Numerous cookbooks of hers remain on my shelf. I usually serve 14 lunches and dinners a week, quite varied, most of them hot, prepared at home, with no frozen dishes. Still, at parties where the talk turns to recipes and food preparation, I can contribute nothing except to repeat that I do not enjoy cooking. Nor do I fancy the over-the-top markets and specialty stores, which are off-putting and overpriced, with their pretensions, their exotic imported edibles in jars, rare spices, and vegetables that look alive.

Finally, as a possible final disqualification, I will admit to what some view as a strange relationship with food. Just read my many poems on fruit, vegetables, olives, cheese, eggs, seafood, and fungi. One acquaintance supposed that I was vegetarian. Not at all; I am from the American West and like beef, lamb, venison, rainbow trout. My approach to foodstuffs is often, however, "problematical," as a literary critic might say. Whether by gustatory pleasure, erotic association, visual fancy, or other cultural connections, the food object takes on an imaginative character comprising but going beyond its utilitarian function; that is, it becomes an idea, embodied. My dislikes (as of eggs and runny cheeses) and strange comparisons, as of mushrooms to flesh of the thigh, appear side-by-side with what is clearly poetic and sensory enjoyment of other dishes. In my poetry, the very feel of the food is suggested, its aura, its resonances and afterimage, so to speak; it takes on something of the metaphysical. (This is possible because, like a still-life painting, it is then material for art, not food.)

All this is connected to embodiment. That the capacity for thought, including thoughts of the invisible and divine, and intimations of immortality, should be attached (and in what manner?) to these bodies of ours passes understanding. Philosophers have paid too little attention to the matter. Sartre is an exception; his fiction and his explicitly philosophical works often overlap at the juncture where he describes the dilemmas of embodiment, making them a cornerstone of his phenomenological system (such as it is) and of his characters' confrontation with the world. Sartre's mode and tone were usually those of disgust (and he was, in my view, a rather disgusting person). In contrast, the novelist and essayist Antoine de Saint-Exupéry, who likewise wrote the body into his work, did so in a much more positive way, as a dimension and instrument of action.

Present-day Occidental society does not overlook the body, certainly. Trillions of dollars have been invested in medical establishments, training of medical personnel, routine care, research, and treatment of those with serious diseases, including those of the mind, since it is viewed by medical practitioners as an extension or organ of the body, not as spirit. Then there are other industries, the over-the-counter drugs and supplements, the weight-loss industry, and those connected to covering, beautification, adornment, or strengthening of face, hair, nails, muscles, and all the rest. The obsession with food as entertainment may, like the beautification industries, be viewed as an attempt to reduce, even deny, bodily realities; certain posh restaurant creations resemble putty or plastic objects, and, like Claiborne's dinner, some gastronomic adventures are merely tastings, barely intended as nourishment.

Notwithstanding these observations, I like to eat; friends will corroborate that. Certain dishes, you understand. The appearance counts too. Color is good; no all-white meals. In that respect, I approve the chefs who serve *crème caramel* with blueberry sauce (though I don't eat custards—read my poem on eggs), or bright red tomato with green asparagus and yellow squash.

De gustibus non est disputandum. It is all a question of taste. Valéry's poems appeal to me by their exquisite choice of words, their unsurpassed craftsmanship, and their refinement of image and what must be called poetic thought. Yet I like also the robust verse of Apollinaire (though he too can be refined). Variety is good, in poetry as in food. But part of taste is proportion—and portions—and taste should be *good* according to "community standards" and one's own. The West Texas cowman J. Evetts Haley was quoted in *Chronicles* as saying that prejudice is a better guide than reason when it comes to eating and art.

I am showing my age; I show also my background, upbringing, ancestral descent. What's wrong with that? I'm my Montreal grandmother's heir. She would not allow watermelon in the house; to her, it was not a suitable food, or a food at all. Are we not all supposed to be ourselves (however they may be understood or redesigned), honor our roots, value individuality—as proposed by pop singer Darin Zanyar: "Be what you wanna be"? *Most* of us, that is—those who aren't guilty by definition (by birth!). My point is not to make final judgments for others. I recognize the individuality—indeed, the idiosyncrasies and eccentricities—of others, their peculiar (in both senses) tastes, the legitimacy of the enormous luxury food business in the United States, and the culinary achievements of some famous chefs. I do not want restaurants to go out of business, chefs and sous-chefs to lose their jobs, waiters to be in the unemployment line. The ideal meal (what a former New Orleans restaurant critic called a "platonic dinner") comprises the best of what nature proposes, circumstances provide or allow, and taste approves. It is subjective, akin to the choices made by love. (Do not, though, use that subjective ideal as a pretext to validate offensive sexual practices.) The old prospector eats with pleasure his can of beans. But the aestheticizing of dinner (along with its valuation on the basis of rarity or strangeness of ingredients) is disproportionate and unfitting to its ends. The "poetry of the table," if one likes that metaphor, is real; but, like verse, it should not be affected, precious. Nor ought we wish to be sated. "Nothing to excess; moderation in all things." Then, *buen provecho, bon appétit*, or, as the current barbarism has it, "Enjoy!"

The APA: Sanctioning the Sexual Abuse of Children

AT ITS MAY 2013 MEETING in San Francisco, the American Psychiatric Association released the fifth edition of the handbook entitled *Diagnostic and Statistical Manual of Mental Disorders.* Among changes from the previous edition was the renaming of what was formerly termed "gender identity disorder." (The American Medical Association uses the term "gender disorder," classifying it as a "serious medical condition.") The new APA label, "gender dysphoria," removes, presumably, the pejorative suggestion of "disorder" and thus pleases the transsexual activists who campaigned for years to get the word expunged and believe, presumably, that the new term is "less pathologizing." Incidentally, *dys-* has the same etymology as *dis-* ("bad," "abnormal"), and *phoria*, from Greek *pherein*, "bear," suggests malaise, in addition. The altered terminology is a result of intense propaganda efforts by outspoken partisans, which are in turn expressions of changed attitudes toward bodies and sexuality—especially the sexualizing of behavior at an early age—and the drive to legitimize these changes and expand their scope. Among the campaigners was WPATH, the World Professional Association for Transgendered Health. Transgenderism has replaced homosexuality as the newest civil-rights frontier. The former Bruce Jenner is among those who have given sex-change cachet, with the panache of athleticism in his case. In the future there will be, doubtless, "no-genderism"—already coming, in fact. A "transitioned" cartoonist, Alison Bechdel, and her girlfriend, Holly Rae Taylor, were in New York in May 2015 for the opening of *Fun Home*, a musical show based on a graphic novel of the same title. (Graphic in more than one way, perhaps.) In an interview, Bechdel said, "We're all queer—there is no normal." Taylor added, "Gender is so passé." Under the administration of Mayor Bill de Blasio, the New York City Commission on Human Rights established in law, as of 2016, the right to be "Gender Non-Conforming" and has made it illegal (with stiff penalties) to enforce gender-inspired grooming standards. Everyone has the right to be called by his "preferred name and pronoun," and to be admitted enthusiastically into the public toilets of his choice.

Among the worst phenomena is the promotion of gender changes in children, including very young ones. It will be noted that "sexual orientation" and "gender identity" are routinely dissociated by many clinicians and other enthusiasts, with the result that what were formerly understood by all as basic categories become slippery and discourse about them difficult. These terms and other new phrasings obscure meaning and facilitate the social androgyny adumbrated above. The trend is a late offshoot of radical feminism and its war against families and their authority—that is, what Simone de Beauvoir called "children's liberation." As Shulamith Firestone wrote in *The Dialectic of Sex: The Case for Feminist Revolution* (1970), "Feminists have to question, not just all of Western culture, but the organization of culture itself, and, further, even the very organization of nature." Beyond the elimination of what she called "male privilege," she wished for the sex distinction itself to be eliminated: "genital difference between human beings would no longer matter culturally."

A documented case is that of Jazz, a boy who "transitioned" as a toddler and, with girl accoutrements and dress, was interviewed by Barbara Walters on *20/20* at age 5 and again at age 12. The child appeared also on *60 Minutes* and was the subject of a documentary that aired on the Oprah Winfrey Network. A YouTube clip on "her" has been viewed, it is said, more than a million times. Adding an hilarious note to the appalling story, one site identifies the "tween" as "possibly the next Dalai Lama."

The interventions for children are of four varieties. First, there is "social transitioning," possible at an early age. Dress, toys, play, changed pronouns, and participation in activities for the other sex (often on a sports team—with ACLU assistance, of course) can mark the alteration. It remains reversible, in theory. Whether reversal can be carried out in practice, and at what cost to the person's psyche, cannot be assessed yet. Early intervention has its fans. According to a video from a series *Not Trans Enough*, transgendered people frequently express regret that they did not transition socially as toddlers and went through puberty in the wrong sex.

Next is hormone therapy, called "puberty blockers." It was first applied to children in Boston in 2009 and has become widespread. There is disagreement on the application, though WPATH has guidelines. Walter J. Meyer III, a psychiatrist and endocrinologist at the University of Texas Medical Branch, observes that not all children who exhibit variances from normal gender behavior are candidates for intervention. They may not be "transgender"; they may be trying out roles, as one mother put it, roles that they will abandon. Other specialists have expressed concern about the unknown long-term effects of hormone therapy for very young people.

Third is upper-body intervention, externally by means of breast-binders or, more radically, by surgery, of two sorts. (One leaves no scars.) Readers will not want to linger over the details, still less over the fourth means of intervention, lower-body redesign for both sexes. WPATH recommends that the latter not be performed on patients younger than 18, whereas upper-body sex-reassignment surgery may be done earlier. One plastic surgeon spoke of her persistent refusal to operate on minors despite parents' pleas, but other "gender confirmation surgeons" do so, and some activists are campaigning for a loosening of the WPATH guidelines. To these means of intervention is added voice therapy, as called for by the condition and age of the patient.

We pay, collectively, for these very costly procedures, financially as well as otherwise. Insurance reimburses many therapies. Among Fortune 500 companies, 25 percent are insured by companies that pay for sex-change operations; children must be among the insurable on family plans. As of a recent count, with the addition of Brown University, 36 colleges have arranged to cover such surgery for their students as well as employees. Yale has considered joining the group, thanks to the pressures of RAGE, the Resource Alliance for Gender Equity.

While the total number of such modifications for children is not reported, it is known that they are carried out widely. How can this be? Public-school counselors (who encourage "individualism" and are often antifamily), teachers, social workers, psychologists and other therapists, medical personnel, members of self-help groups and associations, and other meddlers may present "options" to suggestible youth ("Would you like to . . . ") and thus be active abettors. The Trans-Kid Purple Rainbow Foundation was set up as a resource, and gatherings such as the Philadelphia Trans Health Conference (June 2013) doubtless exercise influence. Alternative schools exist, and others are promoted as "safe and caring," in the words of one Canadian support organization. As the YouTube figure indicates, the internet and social media, to which children generally have unlimited access, are a rich source of encouragement and models. The prestige attached to rebellion leads to aping of other youthful rebels (ironically, a conformist behavior). Television programmers who feature and glamorize young "trans" children bear responsibility, as do viewers, with their complacency and appetite for the outrageous.

Most enabling and most abusive are parents, without whom gender-altering measures could not be taken, obviously; out of caution, even the most radical, lucre-mad, or publicity-seeking endocrinologists and surgeons would not treat children otherwise. Apparently, permissiveness comes easily in families that are disturbed and those where childrearing is conceived as "empowerment." We are to "affirm" children, let them be what they want to be. (A man reported at a conference that at age two his son was "teaching us" "how he wanted to be in the world," and added that he hoped he was not holding him back at age three.) Many parents, of liberal views or weak character, apparently do not dare counter their children's inclinations, however capricious or ill advised, when endorsed by specialists. (Your authority may not be any good, but that of sociologists, psychiatrists, counselors, and other purported experts is.) These adults, far from disinterested, and opposed to traditional paternal status and roles, teach children to call adults by their given names, challenge what they are told, assert their "rights" (no duties), "think for themselves." The Department of Health and Human Services did concede in a pertinent memo that it is difficult for adolescents to "think critically" and that they are often impulsive. While this official acknowledgment encourages society to tolerate dependency and long-postponed adulthood, and also favors jurisprudence that would treat as juveniles those well past adolescence, it may not do much against the trend toward measures of sex modification taken earlier and earlier.

This is Rousseau all over again. "Power to the children!" Parents have, in effect, abdicated responsibility. That they themselves were brought up in an age of permissiveness and have been subject to liberal brainwashing on a huge scale should not relieve them of the charges of child abuse. (One outspoken parent of a "trans" child studied literary theory in graduate school.) Afraid of countering trends, "offending" the "differently abled," and interfering in children's psychic development and freedom, they help them take extraordinary steps with long-term physical and social consequences. As the 19th-century literary critic Charles de Sainte-Beuve could attest if he returned, to live in an abnormally fashioned body is a burden.

In essence, the lunacy just sketched fulfills the vision of Soviet-style social engineers who wish for parents to hand over to social organisms the functions of childrearing; one currently preaching that children "belong to the community" is Melissa Harris-Perry, a host on MSNBC for four years and, I regret to say, at one time a faculty member in political science at my former institution. The abettors of sex changes in children constitute a new class of criminals, whose depredations, made possible by medical techniques, are underpinned by radical social attitudes that have been successfully imposed by strident, aggressive holders of power. To lead a child astray is a terrible deed. A millstone around one's neck, we are told, would be better.

What Are Poems Made Of?

IT MUST BE RECOGNIZED at the outset that the best illustration of what makes a poem is the poem itself. Poetry is a bit like dance; whatever you may say about it—describing the movements or blocking them out as a diagram—will not come close to the real dance, which must be carried out bodily. Words are the body of the poem, without which *there is no poem*. Apart from that fact, there are no givens, no rules, no formulae. (I call the statement a *fact*, because we don't consider grunts, gestures, facial expressions to constitute poems, nor is music by itself the same as poetry, nor painting—despite *ut pictura poesis* and similar expressions of analogies among the arts—nor a garden, however lovely, nor a blank sheet of paper.) Conclusions on what makes a poem must be *ex post facto*, and are, obviously, a function of the poem. Fortunately, it is still legitimate, and possible, to make some general observations, and of some value, if only by way of reminder. The comments to follow apply best to short poems, certainly not to epics and other extended narratives, nor to verse drama. Moreover, they generally are better suited to poetry after 1900 than to older verse.

The great painter Edgar Degas—he who painted horse races, ballet dancers, and scenes in New Orleans—remarked to his friend Stéphane Mallarmé, a Symbolist poet, that he did not understand why he was unable to write a poem. "I've got lots of ideas," he added. Mallarmé replied, "My dear Degas. Poems are made from words, not ideas."

A major dimension of words as they function in verse is their sound, in individual words and combinations. It was noted earlier that the appeal of verbal sound is very deep-set, close to our vital organs. Of course rhyme and strict meter are no longer viewed as essential; even in the distant past, rhyme was omitted in dramatic and narrative blank verse and in the 19th century was not used in some lyrics. But meter and end-rhyme constitute poetic resources, as do assonance, consonance, alliteration, interior rhyme, and irregular stress patterns. Iambic pentameter remains congenial to English-language poets, though other fixed meters, used throughout a poem or introduced here and there, and unusual beats, such as the "sprung rhythm" of Gerard Manley Hopkins, have been used effectively. (The appeal of iambic pentameter and meter in general may be connected to breathing patterns, as Claudel thought, and other internal visceral movements.)

If you call on these features, your poem can get by, perhaps, with fewer additional attributes. One trap of free verse is that, after the traditional verbal features just listed, on which poets long relied, have been discarded, the poet must create his effects with what remains—in order to distinguish his lines from cut-up prose and thus fulfill what may be called "the poetic contract." Good free verse—the sort that will last and one's friends will want to reread—may take exceptional skill.

In addition to sounds, there are other aspects to verbal functioning in poetry—the denotations or dictionary meanings, obviously, and connotations that come from past and present usage. They may include derivations and earlier meanings. Though etymologies prove little, having in mind the derivation adds, for author and reader, interest and flavor. In addition, the context of the words in a line—their mates, so to speak—may shed unusual light on them. The general tone of the poem colors everything. Tone is made up of everything mentioned so far. One of its dimensions is the level of expression: ordinary or erudite, plain or ornate, direct or oblique. Likewise it involves authorial attitudes: respect, sarcasm, humor, familiarity.

To summarize: Verbal choices come from and bear the sense of the poem. Think of that word, *sense*: It is synonymous with *meaning* and *import* but also signifies *sensation*. Nothing illustrates better than a poem the rich overlap between sense as meaning and sense as sensation, or feeling, about which more will be said presently. The word *sense* comes from Middle French or Latin *sens* (< *sensus*, past participle of *sentire*; cognate with German *Sinn*, 'sense,' 'mind'). This connection supposes the link between sense data and understanding.

A further dimension of the poem is its form—that is, form on the page and what (of that) can come across in oral presentation. To be formless is impossible, but for form to be bad, annoying, apparently arbitrary, is frequent. Relying on eccentricities and tricks, such as variety in fonts, unusual capitalization, the scattering of words on the page, or bizarre margins, will not take one far, because no points are awarded for originality, since all this was done in French some 150 years ago by Mallarmé, then particularly well by Apollinaire, followed by many English-language imitators. Anyhow, as experience shows, the product is likely to have little else beyond the eye-catching features. Poems in the shape of what they're about, called ideograms, are not new either: for instance, a poem on rain with the words drizzling in long columns, or an apple poem in the shape of that fruit. Poems printed on cards that the reader shuffles in order to create various combinations may have been created; such a novel was, in French, by Marc Saporta. Form is worth consideration, however; it is a major player. We may apply to poetry the phrase Percy Lubbock applied decades ago to fiction: The best form is that which makes the most of its subject.

So length of line, stanza, and arrangement, separately or together, must either be decided upon initially, dictating then what follows, or will arise in the course of composition. Errors, changes of mind, false starts are frequent. It is good to try to correct them or disguise them or, better, take advantage of them to devise even better lines. From the *work* comes the *work*, said Cage; poetic windfalls can come from the poet's refusing to give in to facility and, instead, forcing what is infelicitous to become better.

Spaces and silences are part of the poem also. Long blocks of lines are discouraging to readers today, while a stanzaic form, with stanzas of varying or identical length, provides "breathers" and may offer a kind of visual rhythm or otherwise contribute to the sense of form. But one must not rely too greatly on space and silence. An illustration is provided by a poem read aloud as part of an "event" held in 2015. The poem concerns a narcotics agent and his dog who are working on the Texas-Mexico border near Laredo. The dog, whose handler and friend has been shot, whines and whines; he ceases when he realizes the man is dead. The poet, who shall be nameless here, paused every few words, presumably to give emphasis to the phrase; that is, she punctuated the lines with blank moments. She . . . punctuated . . . the lines . . . with . . . silences. That's a facile tactic to dramatize the contents. It didn't work. Very touching; but it wasn't a poem; it was just a prose bit worked into "poetry" by significant pauses.

All that about verbal elements and form is very good; there's no need to take back a word of it, except by acknowledgment that, despite everything, poems *do* have content of some sort. Valéry, a disciple of Mallarmé, emphasized how the sound and the meaning of words play off against or with each other and with our poetic sensibility. He recounted how one of his most admired poems was born out of a rhythm in his head that kept coming at him and, in time, assumed other characteristics of sound, perhaps fitting obscurely something in his psyche; ultimately they led to a decision on line length, stanzas, and development of potential. The resulting product, "The Cemetery by the Sea," is full of ideas; it's really a philosophical poem. Numerous poets of renown, even Modernist ones such as Eliot, have set out to write on certain topics, chosen beforehand, about which they had ideas, that is, thoughts, or on which they had perspectives, at least.

So one must agree that the finished poem, if there is one, will be a marriage of words and thoughts or something similar. Gide spoke of the "gift of being moved by plums," and Williams did an impromptu little lyric, a gem, on that very fruit. Critics speak of "themes" in literature, such as marriage, death, or happiness, or something modest such as a bright morning. To write a poem on any one of these themes involves inevitably one's "thoughts."

Here, once again, an acknowledgment must be made of the absurd claims put forth by the late Derrida and others who assert that, since definitions are circular (mutually self-referential), words have no absolute reference; there are just competing fictions. Language, that is, cannot represent reality; it represents itself. This is nonsense. Speech *is* functional and conveys meaning, willy-nilly. Ideation occurs spontaneously and immediately. (Surely, I suggested earlier, when Derrida and his ilk took their prescription pills, they probably read the label and took two, as indicated. Still, he had the gall to maintain that others' words did not have firm meaning; yet, he averred, *his* did.) Words, even prepositions such as *for* and *by*, cannot be separated from their denotation except in extraordinary use (senseless repetitions, for instance—and even then some sense usually survives), so that what the word designates will be present at least as an aura, a feeling, a shadow. *Doughnut* does not have the same resonances as *alligator*.

Poetic "contents" are usually, however, not statements, or at least not reducible to statements alone, but something more subtle, often oblique—suggestions, savor. Poetry thrives on indirection—a certain *slant* of light, as Dickinson wrote. Concepts and thoughts may lie well below the surface, almost invisible, cloaked in images. By *image* is meant something perceptible, usually visual, described verbally—for instance, a table set for coffee, in the sunlight—or else a figure of speech, chiefly a simile or metaphor (itself calling up tangible things), which, by analogy, evokes a perception. The word *idea* comes through Latin from the Greek ιδεαν (*idean*, 'to see'). Images are sometimes called *correlatives* or "objective correlatives," after Eliot's use of the term. Ideas may be obscure, although too much obscurity kills the poem. But readers no longer look for didacticism in verse, though Ralph Waldo Emerson insisted upon it and Shelley, it will be recalled, declared that poets were "the unacknowledged legislators of the world." That was before Poe, in his essay "The Poetic Principle," banished instruction as foreign to the spirit of poetry. "A poem should not mean / But be," wrote Archibald MacLeish in his "Ars poetica." Eliot's verse is full of cultural, moral, and religious judgments; but then Eliot, Modernist though he was early and at midpoint in his career, became an archconservative and is widely viewed as a fossil, with totalitarian leanings to boot. (So be it, in critical circles; his Nobel Prize, his plays, and his *Four Quartets* will stand.)

To recapitulate: Praising goodness or stating one's convictions no longer works very well. One would-be contributor to the poetry pages of *Chronicles* repeatedly submits lines crammed with his personal beliefs. The latter are not dishonorable, but, alas, they are of interest chiefly to him, and not in the least poetic, since he does not have the skill to avoid prosaic declarations. As Gide observed, it's with good convictions that one makes bad literature. Much protest poetry today is simply complaining. Welty, readers will recall, wrote that "the zeal to reform, which quite properly inspires the editorial, has never done [literature] much good." The journalist Edwin M. Yoder is among present-day writers who advise against putting moral or political judgments into poetry.

In addition, a poet's aim will not be to convey information as such. One does not want to read verse that summarizes the weather patterns, or describes a polygon, or states who was in the president's Cabinet in 1900. Longer forms may *tell* a great deal, such as the book-length verse novel, *Ludlow* (2007), by David Mason, concerning a 1914 labor dispute and massacre, or the sequence of poems "Acadie du nord," by Darrell Bourque, in his 2013 collection *Megan's Guitar*, which recounts imaginatively, by means of separate poems, the 18th-century Acadians' experience. Even then the sequence cannot be reduced to an historical account. In shorter forms, poets may include interesting bits of trivia and insights, but their purpose is generally to touch and move readers, not to relay facts.

Where does feeling enter into this picture? Feeling is *emotion* as well as *sensation*; the sensation is a sign of the emotion. Valéry said that poetry was "the attempt to represent, or reinstitute, by articulated language" the thing or things that sighs, tears, cries, caresses, and other reactions express somatically (through the body). Did Wordsworth not define poetry as "the spontaneous overflow of powerful feelings," its origin being "emotion recollected in tranquility"? (About the "spontaneous" quality more could be said another time.) Perhaps Degas had, in addition to ideas, feelings that he would have liked to put into words. Cheeriness, desire, sorrow, joy, melancholy, regret may appear to be the stuff of poetry. "Our sweetest songs are those that tell of saddest thought," wrote Shelley in "To a Skylark." But the poet's role is better understood not as experiencing feeling, or achieving the poetic state, but making others experience it. For that, feeling does not suffice, as was remarked earlier in this book. "Everyone has been happy and unhappy," Valéry noted; but to *feel* does not imply to *make felt* (that is, to make others feel), and, still less, "*beautifully* felt." Thus one cannot get by simply with saying "I'm sad" or "I feel wonderful." He goes on: "All the passions of the world, all the incidents of a lifetime, even the most moving, are incapable of producing the least line of fine poetry." For this, poetic tactics, including suitable sound effects and images, must be used.

Can anger make up a poem? Yes, but it's tricky. Yeats said that of our quarrel with others, we make rhetoric (speeches, articles, letters to the editor), whereas poetry is made out of our quarrel with ourselves (conflicts, deep dissatisfactions, profound ennui, hatred of the self). Perhaps slanted ire and resentment, bent in the direction of sarcasm and satire, are most effective. Pope was good at that.

What about melancholy, lethargy, boredom? Great poets have made great poems with those tones and topics (Keats, Baudelaire), but the average scribbler cannot achieve it. Self-indulgence, poetic or psychological, does not by itself go far. Brautigan's lines titled "At the California Institute of Technology," quoted earlier, are a case in point.

There is another aspect to the functioning of poetry: the role of the listener or reader, emphasized in recent decades by what is called reader-reception criticism. It has been argued that the work always exists in a triangular relationship that includes, besides the text, the author (in the original context of production) and the reading public; the latter, individually and collectively, contributes to the functioning of the text. Reading (and listening) suppose the ability to understand; as part of that, one brings, inevitably, a context, suitable expectations, and the willingness to think poetically or "suspend disbelief" (as Coleridge put it, with a different emphasis). Those who deal with and are to appreciate poetry must have a sort of "availability" that provides a good field for the poem to work in. Might this foreknowledge or predisposition define too narrowly the range for approach? Do readers understand only that which they have understood already? Not by any means; strangeness is one of the attractions of the poetic art.

Three further observations may be added. First, one should beware of relying excessively on dreams for the substance of poetry. Jungian and Freudian analysis of the irrational belongs elsewhere, if anywhere; generally, poems are fabrications of the conscious mind. ("Kubla Khan" gives an idea of exceptions to the rule.) Second, while poetry may be shocking, and even written for that purpose, its essence cannot be to shock. The strange, the eerie may have appeal, and can last; but what shocks today will shock no longer next year, and when that balloon has been deflated it will crash, if there is nothing else. Third, to cultivate simply the antithesis of what has been done before is not very productive. By the way, iconoclasts need to be familiar with the tradition to overturn it; iconoclasm supposes dialogue, intertextuality.

With the foregoing remarks in mind, one may ask again, "What are poems made of?" The field is vast, anything and everything. That includes, obviously, the poet's self and autobiography, but it is better to cast one's nets elsewhere, at least sometimes, given that Walt Whitman already wrote *Song of Myself* and countless confessional poets from the 1950's and on have spilled out their experiences, miseries, or arrogance on the page. Think of other things.

This other material may come from experience, whether it be everyday or exceptional. Teachers and critics often advise, appropriately, "Write about what you know." One implication of that advice is to avoid the academic. The great Southwestern stylist Mary Austin noted, "Intimacies . . . between land and the people breed poets faster, and much better ones, than do universities." Yet to do a successful poem on a topic does not mean that the poet must have direct, personal knowledge of it. Authentic knowledge and understanding may come through reading, then analogizing, using the imagination. The New Orleans novelist Shirley Ann Grau pointed out that imagination is the essence of literature; the position that you can write only what you know intimately would turn literature "into nothing more than autobiography."

For instance, the present writer has published quite a number of poems about war or set in wartime, from the campaigns of Alexander the Great through the Mexican and Franco-Prussian wars, the two world wars, and the American conflict in Vietnam; three prison-camp poems are in this group. Yet she never witnessed combat, nor was she a prisoner of war; but enormous reading permitted her to imagine the experiences. Bourque was not alive in the 18th century, but he was able to call on numerous written sources and perhaps oral ones and imagine the time and scenes. Two poets writing today, both women, A.E. Stallings and Constance Rowell Mastores, even have poems dealing with the Trojan War, a topic some 3,000 years old and mediated now through countless other poems in numerous languages. Was Coleridge really acquainted with the Ancient Mariner?

Readers may appreciate sample passages illustrating certain points just made. The quotations are drawn from various sorts of poems treating a range of themes. Though much can be said in favor of indirection in art, it is useful that these passages are plain enough to be appreciated at first reading; they will serve as the conclusion to this essay. Here's a passage by Mona Lisa Saloy, from her poem "Roots, 200 Years, Louisiana Purchase," in *Red Beans and Ricely Yours*. The poem, simple and direct, relies on enumerations and local color:

> It was 1803, New Orleans, world port,
> ....
> Third largest U.S. city, best land deal
> for four cents an acre, American,
> but France plus Spain, Latin roots now Creole
> when baked African spice spills in Vieux Carré
> Faubourgs, below Canal, downtown music,
> shotgun homes, brick walkways, lamb's ear gardens . . .

This is history, including city development and ethnic components, but it is also urban atmosphere, with names and other details to evoke the neighborhoods below Canal Street. Listeners need to bring something of their own to the poem, however; if readers had never heard of New Orleans or knew nothing of Louisiana history, they would be less likely to respond well. Note that judgments are missing. If readers wish, they may draw conclusions for themselves. In another poem, "Louisiana Log," Saloy again uses enumeration, with numerous characteristic elements: foodstuffs, parades, music, bayous, graveyards. These poems, based on reading and lived experience, illustrate compatibility between the poet and the topic; the reader or listener senses on the poet's part not only familiarity but appreciation. Yet she does not use the first person at all.

Then there is nature, a source of poetic materials from the Greeks to the present. Here is a recent example from Mastores, drawn from her collection *A Deep But Dazzling Darkness.* It will be noted that the evocation of the tree involves relatively little description, leaning rather on imagination, personal response, and suggestions from the past. The tree is a correlative of something else, not quite stated. The poem is called "Legend of the Deodar Cedar" (Himalayan Cedar).

> Bark encrusted in silver,
> crackled, broken into parts,
> what language do you speak to me
> in this moment of hearing?
> ....
>
> I observe you in the morning,
> but fall in love with you toward dusk,
> when your hoary pillar soars
> and disappears into the fog and filtered light.

The poem continues with a reference to the Tristan legend (as used by Wagner, for instance):

> Quiet and unshielded, I await your word,
> your telling of me to myself,
> who am isolate without a story;
> ....
> who am Isolde before the scene with Tristan . . .

And here's an extract from a poem entitled "Wasps," from *Noble Savage*, by James Adams:

Red wasps, flying in the grass,
Folding their wings
....
By their faces like curtains
....
Brown wasps, what do they see
As they paper maché [*sic*]
        their young to a tree
Their world's upside down
twenty feet from the ground.

Here are lines, with striking sound patterns, from a poem in tercets called "The Blue of the Bay," by Mason.

What can be learned from the blue of the bay
I do not know, I cannot say,
the stone of the sand on the shore by the bay.

The bird on its back lying dead on the shore,
its breast torn open, its hollow core—
what more can be learned of the bird on the shore?

If someone is crying, I cannot hear,
and if I am crying inside I fear
no one will hear, no one will hear.

That leads easily to the subject of death. In Paul Lake's collection *The Republic of Virtue* there is a poem that has an "idea" on death; but it is rendered well as a scene. It's called "First Fruit," identified as "the bitterest." By that biblical image the poet sets a solemn tone; yet the setting is ordinary. He continues:

. . . It's not my son
with seven-year-old wisdom
discussing death around the kitchen table,
naming who will die
in chronological order down to him,
with an actuary's emotionless precision,

but my daughter's first unseasoned cry,
"But is my *Daddy* going to die?"

Here's a different treatment: death avoided. The poem, a sonnet called "A Postcard From Greece," is by Stallings. It is printed as a 14-line block, an effective arrangement. There are irregular rhymes. It begins as a car, skidding, is about to crash down a slope into the Aegean Sea. By good fortune, it is stopped before it plunges. Here are the concluding lines:

Somehow we struck an olive tree instead.
Our car stopped on the cliff's brow. Suddenly safe,
We clung together, shade to pagan shade,
Surprised by sunlight, air, this afterlife.

A Road Trip to Charleston

LIKE MANY UNDERTAKINGS, the travels recounted here had not one principal aim but two, even three; an original purpose develops shoots and branches and becomes a veritable tree of intentions. This very book, consisting of comments on literature, manners, education, and so forth, on the one hand, and personal reminiscences, on the other, is two-headed. In the matter I am about to relate, the purposes derived from personal connections and interests, thence from chance. First, some background to illuminate these connections.

In 2003 I attended for the first time a meeting, held that year in New Orleans, of the John Randolph Club, sponsored by The Rockford Institute. The powwows start on a Friday evening with a reception and address; they last through a black-tie banquet and debate on Saturday evening, comprising in between talks on various social and political topics. Often the hotel selected for the gathering is an historic one. The membership is not monolithic; there is a range of political and religious opinions, some expressed, some held quietly. Foreign affairs compose part of the discussion program always. The foolish and horrible wars launched in recent years and the unjustified, expensive, and dangerous presence of the United States military branches in all parts of the world are among recurring topics. The point is not to offend others—though plenty of others offend us—but to support certain verities, spur listeners' consciences, examine current matters, and propose remedies for social ills. The editors of *Chronicles: A Magazine of American Culture* also get together as a group.

I liked the meeting so well that I've attended most yearly events since, and, now that I'm married again, Patric accompanies me. In November 2010, the gathering was held in Charleston, South Carolina; we decided to drive there rather than to fly. Pat, who's been on six continents, had never visited Charleston; this was a fine opportunity. I knew the city somewhat—its beautiful location, its architecture, manners, and history—but this visit would extend my acquaintance. That being decided, we thought we would take in Savannah also—another city Pat had not seen, though I had been there, briefly. (It reminded me of New Orleans, with the addition of bluffs along the river.) Earlier, Savannah had come to a rather ghoulish national attention with the publication in 1994 of John Berendt's semifictional *Midnight in the Garden of Good and Evil.* I was interested principally in the urban design of Savannah (the squares), the domestic architecture, setting on the river bank, shipping, and trees.

The city is connected also to three figures who interest me: John Wesley, who arrived there with his brother Charles in 1736 and left precipitously at the end of the following year; Juliette Gordon Lowe, the founder of the Girl Scouts, whose birthplace in Savannah we visited; and Julien Green (1900-1998), a French novelist, or, better put, a Southern Gothic novelist who wrote in French. He was born in Paris but of Southern antecedents; his grandfather built a famous Savannah house before the 1861-65 war. I must mention also Savannah native Johnny Mercer. To read of John Wesley's unhappy stay in Savannah, one can conclude that the young settlement was already a garden of good and evil. Despite outward piety, or perhaps because of it, he seemed to attract controversy and adversaries. On the counsel of a Moravian from a group he had known on shipboard, who advised that he should avoid further contact with female admirers, he spurned a woman whom he had apparently courted. She was the niece of one of his opponents. She then married another. Given Wesley's local influence, they eloped to South Carolina. Upon their return, Wesley refused to give her communion. He was sued by the husband for indirect defamation of character. The outcome of the jury deliberations was a mistrial. The townspeople were said to be "divided" in their opinions. It became clear that he should leave town.

Our third destination would be Macon, Georgia, where I have a friend. He has himself told how we met, so I can repeat the story here. In the late 1990's, when I was still in New Orleans, I lived in a mid-rise condominium building on Second Street at St. Charles Avenue, in the Garden District. Readers of my poetry will recall evocations of various scenes visible from my windows (such as "Sunset"—consisting, since my place faced northeast, of cloud reflections from brilliant sun opposite—"New Orleans: The Winter Hour," and "Rooftops," a post-Katrina poem). The building is well suited for Mardi Gras activities; almost all the parades proceed, or straggle, along St. Charles, and many residents can see parades from their living rooms or balconies. Public rooms on the ground floor of the building open into a small garden on the St. Charles side, protected by a stout forged-iron fence with no gate. If one doesn't want to wander up and down the avenue, the garden—a patch of dirt and grass with a few bushes—is a good choice for parade-watching; one is allowed to take out folding chairs, and no one, even small children and old people, can be trampled. Guests are allowed.

In the two public rooms giving access outside, residents may set up tables for their own private buffets. (These parades are all-day or all-evening events.)

It is understood that one doesn't poach on others' territory, and thus red beans and rice in a casserole, chips, cheese, wine and beer, and so on can be left while the hosts run out to see the next floats. One year, a Mercer University history professor I'll call Jack was staying during Carnival weekend in a condo belonging to an absent acquaintance. Earlier that day, he had probably had a long lunch and several glasses of wine at Gallatoire's or the Louisiana Purchase Kitchen, and perhaps a few drinks at cocktail time elsewhere. He has a keen appetite for Louisiana food, and he always enjoys a good bourbon or the fruit of the vine. Returning to the building, and walking through the public rooms en route to the garden, he found what he supposed to be a party for the residents and guests in general. He innocently helped himself to red beans set out by my friend Elizabeth and her son (a wonderful cook) for their family. Then Jack poured himself some wine from their table. This much he remembers.

What occurred next is not entirely clear, but Elizabeth must have encountered him at the table. Gracious though she is, she may have observed it was a private spread. Jack would have apologized profusely, and he is so genuine, so likeable that even a misanthrope I knew appreciated him. During their conversation, Elizabeth somehow found out that he spoke French. Neither she nor Jack recalled later how the topic came up; why would she have inquired about his foreign-language skills? However the conversation may have proceeded, she then led him out to the garden, knowing I was there, and introduced him to me by saying, "This man speaks French." (True: He does, preferably though with only one interlocutor at a time. He also has Russian and practical and scholarly German.) Very good. We like to be courteous in New Orleans, so I asked him, in French, whether he was from Paris. No, he replied in the same language. "*Vous êtes français, cependant*?" No. Perhaps he was a Québécois, then? Or Belgian, Swiss? Startled, doubtless, by these rapid-fire questions in French, he finally blurted out, "Hell, no, I'm from South Carolina." His Deep South accent supported that claim amply. I didn't test him on his French. We quickly learned that we had much in common—he has a scholarly interest in World War I, for instance, as do I—and when he took me to lunch the next day (another lengthy New Orleans meal), we discovered even more. We remain friends to this day.

In 2002 he arranged for me to be invited to Mercer, in Macon, to give two lectures, remunerated modestly; he put me up in his guest room, took me around, introduced me to colleagues and some bridge-playing friends, and held two dinner parties in my honor. In 2008, when I did a poetry reading at Macon State, again Jack was my host. Having learned of our trip to the southeast in November 2010, he invited us to Macon and arranged another presentation for me. Pat and I would stay at his house; he would, once more, give dinner parties, and I'd speak to his history students by way of reading and commenting on some of my historically based poems.

So Pat and I had chosen our destinations. I drove, along a route I'd mapped out, which took us first along I-10 (and I-12 in southeastern Louisiana) to Gulfport, Mississippi. The next day we went on to Mobile, with its bay and causeways, from which one sees the USS *Alabama*, then into the Florida Panhandle, with which Pat was not familiar, and late in the day to southern Georgia. These drives were pleasurable; the weather was good, the coastal scenes attractive, the pine forests thick. On the third day, we reached Savannah easily, in time to wander from our hotel through the port area and see the river.

"Wander" is a manner of speaking. Pat, already then in his 80's, has congestive heart failure, bad knees (from 60 years of tennis), and poor balance. He doesn't just stroll along like a sightseer. We look ahead and plan our steps every few yards in order to minimize effort and risk. Old Savannah has cobblestones, uneven walkways, and high curbs; and it is congested, like the French Quarter. So we moved carefully. Tourist shops don't interest me, but I was pleased to see the port. The next day, we took two tours on "trolleys"; there was some duplication of itinerary, but that was all right. One can get off the bus, look around, and get on the next one. We stopped at the famous Pirates' House, said to be the oldest structure in Georgia. Many sailors were shanghaied there or nearby; a convenient web of tunnels facilitated the operation, and they may have been used later by the Underground Railroad.

Now, these tours on foot and bus may have been hard on Pat; we left the bus on several occasions to walk a bit, looking more closely at a neighborhood or an historic site. Sometimes I overestimate his endurance; he may do so himself. The half-day's drive to Charleston the next morning was lovely—the trees still had their leaves of dark autumnal colors, especially in the low coastal areas—and he enjoyed the ride; but he was probably fatigued. At the John Randolph Club reception that evening, held on an open terrace, in weather just barely cool, he shivered so, even in a good wool jacket, that he had to leave. He did not participate in the architectural walking tours, though at lunchtime on Saturday we walked through the historic commercial district, looking at galleries and antique shops. I suppose he got wearier than we realized; on the way back, as by plan I went ahead, he turned in the wrong direction and went well out of his way before reaching our hotel. For the Saturday banquet, he dressed in a fancy bow tie, matching cummerbund, and fine green jacket—his Irish formal attire. But he had to rise from the table before dessert. It was clear that he wasn't well.

In the past he had other serious illnesses, even crises: a collapsed lung (1956), emboli lodged in his lungs, which nearly killed him (1964) and from which he recovered slowly; bladder cancer; a heart attack (2004) caused by a huge thrombosis. It is good that we'd appreciated the scenery en route to Savannah and Charleston, for during the remainder of the journey he could enjoy little. After the JRC meeting, we arrived in Macon on Sunday afternoon at 4:00 or so. Jack had not yet returned from a luncheon-and-bridge party, but he'd left the back door open for us. As I started with our gear along the path from his driveway, I heard a thud and a yell from Pat. He was stretched out his full length, on his back, on the drive. The car door had swung slightly on the inclined pavement and had hit him on his blind side, like a defender tackling a quarterback.

We were to stay in the guest room upstairs. But Pat thought that he could not climb the steps. Jack arranged a bed for him on the living-room couch. That evening, the Mercer dean, the dean's wife, and one other couple came to dinner. Thoroughly ill by then, Pat remained on the sofa, covered with blankets, coughing, and going from shivers to fever and back. Jack served drinks in the den (the favorite spot anyhow), with the sick man on the other side of the wall. We dined in a separate dining room. A kitchen helper took food to Pat, but he could not eat much. I slept upstairs that night but the next night transferred to another sofa, providential, in the den, and kept the door open to be within earshot of him. Late on Monday he managed to get up, out of social duty, so he could accompany me to visit friends connected to Macon State, but we could not stay long. During the remainder of our visit he did not leave the sofa, except to use the downstairs facilities, and that with difficulty: He fell four times while trying to get up and walk.

After my talk on Tuesday, Jack held a second dinner party, a large one, with a vast quantity of delicious hot dishes served buffet style. I recall that the next-door neighbor, who was there with his wife, helped Pat to go to the bathroom, with the cook holding him on the other side. The situation was explained to everyone, and, with Pat's permission, numerous guests went to Pat's side to visit with him, like courtiers of Louis XIV attending his levée. One couple was particularly concerned: The wife was a retired nurse and, I thought, full of wise comments. She could not persuade him, however, to seek medical attention in Macon.

Why, one may wonder, didn't I insist that he do so? Jack has spent his whole scholarly career in Macon and knows everyone worth knowing, including doctors. He would have helped get us into a hospital somehow. But Pat refused. Perhaps he thought he would get stuck in Macon. He would not allow me to cancel the talk scheduled at Mercer and leave prematurely. All we did was telephone to his Houston doctor to make an appointment for the day after our return. That last night on the den sofa I hardly slept because

Pat was in such distress in the next room, feverish, coughing. Thanking Jack profusely and with words of gratitude also to his neighbors and friends, we left the next morning to drive to Gulfport. The passenger seat reclines well, and Pat could make himself moderately comfortable; he did better that day than one would have expected.

The nighttime, again at the Gulfport hotel, was not easy, and it took a long while for Pat to rise the next morning, get dressed, and do the minimum necessary to get himself to the car. He was gray. I asked whether we should stop in New Orleans or Baton Rouge—large cities on the way, familiar to me. No, he wanted to get back to Houston. There is such a thing, doubtless, as smelling home. Exhausted, we arrived in the dark of early evening. When the doctor saw him the next day, he ordered an X-ray, which confirmed the diagnosis he'd already reached: double pneumonia. I drove Pat to the hospital without delay; he was there for five nights, a long stay by present standards, and he was not distinctly better for six weeks or so. The doctor told him to remain at home and especially avoid his and other doctors' offices—too many sick people. "Fragile" was the man's word to describe Pat, even after he was supposedly well.

Have we given up road travel? Certainly not. Each summer we drive from Houston across Texas—the longer way, perhaps, *via* El Paso (to see friends there), or the route closer to an hypotenuse, *via* the Panhandle—thence into New Mexico and Colorado. We've had side trips from our Colorado Springs residence: to Santa Fe for the opera, to Taos for a concert, to Chaco Canyon, to the North Rim of the Grand Canyon, to the Grand Junction area, to northern Colorado, southern Wyoming, and eastern Utah. We've driven frequently to Louisiana and various Texas destinations not too far away. In 2012 we went to Ohio for a scholarly colloquium, drove west to St. Louis (Pat's home city), and thence to Colorado.

Why all this moving about? Why not avoid distraction, as Pascal suggested, and learn to stay (more or less) in a closed room? Or, short of that, at least stay home? Why try, in Baudelaire's metaphor, to run from one hospital bed to another in this sick ward, the world? My friend Martha Mackenzie reported that she heard a man say to his wife, as they were going into a reception, "We have a nice home, Denise. Why don't we ever stay there?" Beauvoir tells of an ancient conqueror who, recounting what he had accomplished and what he intended for the future, added, "Then I shall rest." He was asked: "Why not rest immediately?" We could emulate my late cat and sleep 16 hours or so each day, playing occasionally, musing, munching, and traveling only upon duress. We could read Augustus J.C. Hare's *Memorials of a Quiet Life*.

Well, projection forward and action on the world—for good (personal or general) or less good—is the human impulse. Begging Pascal's pardon, I'll say that only an idiot wants to remain in quietude, silent, immobile. (Pascal was not well and died young.) Or a monk long trained in prayer and contemplation of holy things. That rules out both of us. Infants reach out to touch what's near; walking, we fall forward; we extend our hands and seize distance with our eyes; Alexander the Great goes to the end of the known earth—and wishes for more worlds to conquer. Ludic activity, starting with children's play, is a privileged sort of action, having no aims beyond itself (and, in the case of sports, good health); and most of the drives Pat and I make are that—play.

All this brings to mind my grandmother and grandfather. After Grandfather retired as a practicing physician in 1933, he and Grandmother took three long journeys by train and ship: a circumnavigation of Africa, the first leg being a train ride by Pullman from Denver to the port of Baltimore; another voyage, to Peru; a third to New Zealand and Japan. Even before the United States entered the war, such travels ended. In September 1939 my Aunt Mary was in France, just completing a summer of piano study at the American Conservatory. With difficulty, she managed to get home. After that, no one went abroad until the war ended. After 1945, Grandmother returned by train at least once to Quebec, and in 1946 she and my aunts drove to Mexico. Since she was born in 1864, she was over 80 at the time. There were numerous family trips to the mountains also—to stay at Grandmother's cabin or go farther afield and higher. On one occasion, she went to San Francisco to see her eldest son. A daughter-in-law criticized the plan, observing to her husband that Grandmother might die on the train. His reply was pointed: "She'd be as willing to die on a Union Pacific train as anywhere else."

By the time of Grandmother's death (not in a railroad car) at the end of 1952, Grandfather, nearly 90, knew that, because of his weakening heart, he should no longer cross the high passes of the Continental Divide (11,500 feet or more). Instead, Aunt Flora drove him occasionally north to Laramie and thence via tolerable elevations to various westerly locations. Years later, my aunts made plans to return to France with me and my daughter; Aunt Flora wanted especially to visit Navarre. She died before summer came. She had, at least, enjoyed the prospect of the adventure.

So may we all—my friends and readers—be pleased with our prospects as long as possible. In later years we may need to extend these prospects vicariously. Before his death, my grandfather had *Richard III* open on his desk; my father (who died, unfortunately, much younger) had embarked on reading *War and Peace*. Think of the short lives of that last Yorkist king (and some of his enemies), of certain characters in that novel. (Some observers might think, however, that Tolstoy's was not short enough.) But did these figures perhaps live more intensely, so deeply and dramatically that little would have been left for them? I doubt it, despite the suggestion made by Camus that one should die "despairing," having had so many experiences and such full ones that nothing more could be hoped for. That's rhetoric, an invitation to seek and embrace as much of the world as possible. We cannot, in any case, assess the inner quality of a life (though often we guess at it); but Camus was right to suggest that one can at least gauge its quantity. That's how Meursault, the hero of *The Stranger*, insists an existence should be judged; he points out, reasonably enough, that to die at 30 is not the same as dying at 70.

Acting on this principle, Pat and I have taken lengthy cruises to South America and to Southeast Asia, the latter starting in Southampton, and have continued our peregrinations through the Southwest and Rocky Mountain areas. Whatever is claimed by global commerce and communication enthusiasts, the planet has not shrunk, nor does Antarctica seem nearby. Seize the day.

Secure of Private Right

"For who can be secure of private right,
If sovereign sway may be dissolved by might?"
—Dryden, *Absalom and Achitophel*

JOHN DRYDEN'S QUESTION, posed more than 300 years ago, supposes a just distinction but also a connection between one kind of rights, which he calls "private," and another, "sovereign sway," or legitimate public order. The public is duly the respecter and guarantor of the private. This does not imply priority of the sovereign state, or the public, nor of some overbearing Rousseauesque "general will," by turns custodial and tyrannical, the tyranny introduced (in socialist states) by means of that very custodianship. Indeed, privacy—that is, the personal—is prior, yielding in matters of legitimate common concern but never a prerogative granted by the state. Garret Keizer has argued that privacy is an essential human value, founded on "creaturely resistance to being used against one's will."

If, however, public right, vulnerable to disorder, can be undone by uncontrolled ambition and abuse of power, security in the private realm is jeopardized. Whatever form one chooses to give to the notion of *sovereign*—unless it is seen as sheer force, which is the antithesis of order as Dryden understood it—a properly ordered public polity is the foundation for privacy, which (among other meanings) Webster's defines as "freedom from unauthorized oversight or observation." Such restraints on the power of the sovereign, as a protection of long-established rights and privileges held by the individuals and institutions that constitute society, were made clear in the Magna Carta (albeit with a very restricted application) and its legacy; the principles were long understood in American jurisprudence.

With respect to government, there are two sides to the privacy coin—government both offending our privacy and defending it. The current federal government, nearly all-knowing and very powerful, is an abusive distortion of the original "sovereign" or authority in America, first that of the separate British colonies (and, behind them imperfectly, England) and then of the federation which they subsequently established. The weakening of the states' constitutional authority by means of increase in federal power, which began in the 19th century and raged through the 20th, continues apace. Federal might is so overgrown that, like an autoimmune disease or a cancer, it has attacked itself (that is, other branches and agencies) through rival bureaucracies and especially the courts. Governmental might, then, especially at the national level, is the enemy. There is a tremendous erosion in data privacy, defined on one website as "the ability of an individual to exercise appropriate control over their [*sic*] personally identifiable information"; in many places, it is considered a "fundamental right." Well, we shall remember Mr. Clinton: All that depends on the meaning of *is*, or *appropriate*, or *fundamental*.

Yet as private rights have been eroded, certain statutes, such as the 1974 Family Privacy Act and its Buckley Amendment, have, in principle at least, protected information formerly disregarded by law, and consequently served our private interests. Thus the student alone can give permission for his university record to be examined by anyone other than the proper officials and himself; you can't get elected to Phi Beta Kappa if you don't sign a waiver allowing the chapter members to examine your transcript. I suspect that the changing student expectations of the 1960's, a decade when many revolted against authority (parental and civil) and ran from the law, were one driving force of this measure. What parents, paying the bills usually, were to know was up to the student.

Nor can our medical facts or records be given out (we are told) without our consent. People used to be quarantined for dread and contagious diseases; nowadays you dare not inquire even whether an applicant for a position might have a communicable or debilitating illness. In some states, vital records are similarly protected. How is it then that at age 65 one gets in the mail a huge number of advertisements for life insurance for "seniors," Medicare advantage plans, supplemental health insurance, electric scooters, free testing for deafness, and so on? To whom, exactly, was my birthdate given out, in such a way that the information was then spread and those using it reached out and touched me like jellyfish tentacles? Ah, my age is a matter of public record; the offending sales staff must have looked up my poet's biography! Still, it doesn't happen to me alone. As one blogger noted, "In this day and age of the internet, privacy is a thing of the past."

Though these insurance advertisements are, if you will, a matter of no great importance, one should remain suspicious of such lists, which can easily be disseminated and misused. Their nuisance value, moreover, is considerable, especially when such advertising clogs the mail along with yet new notices from banks assuring me that my account and credit-card information is safe in their hands (of which I remain assured by no means). One can endure telephone solicitations from representatives of what purport to be good causes, and, despite the "Do Not Call" restriction, for commercial services such as roof repair. Still, whose business might it be whether I own my residence outright or not? The bank's, perhaps, and no one else's. Nor is it, I suppose, truly dreadful—just offensive to good manners—that I must call out my birthdate in the pharmacy line in order to get my prescription. I've become a date, not a name nor even a number, since Social Security numbers, having been used for criminal purposes, are now considered confidential.

Numerous federal measures of dubious constitutionality—extraordinary by any reasonable standard—are presently taken in the name of national security, to which private right, we are told, must be sacrificed. If our foreign and domestic policies were what they should be—if we made fewer enemies and dealt suitably (promptly, firmly) with those we have within our borders, just across, and overseas—then such measures could be reduced or eliminated. Not likely, is it? Moral protection of the public is alleged meanwhile as justification for various local measures. Coaches in the Little League in a New Jersey township and anyone connected peripherally to that association, even concession employees, must now be fingerprinted. Try, however, to get your local librarians or school officials to remove obviously offensive material from shelves where children can browse, and you'll be accused of censorship. Meanwhile, register for this and that, with pin or password or a ten-digit number, have your money transfers examined, show your ID (whether authentic, as mine is, or counterfeit), and get yourself X-rayed at the airport. Woe, however, to the polling-place official who challenges certain voters' cards, or a sheriff who, when dealing with real threats, demands proper identification.

What is equally unsettling is the phenomenon by which Americans have lost so much privacy of the sort that is connected to personhood. They barely know what such privacy is, and they do not know what they have lost. This is a moral matter with social aspects. The more your privacy is invaded routinely from childhood on, the less you will understand about what is "appropriate" for others and what should be reserved for yourself. How much spying should we tolerate? In the new AltSchools [*sic*], in California and New York, every classroom action and word is captured by electronic fisheye lenses embedded in the walls. And on the internet your location, your browsing records, the sites you visit may be reported, may they not, to advertisers and meganetworks with far-flung tentacles? What personal questions should those in a position of influence ask? Should the bank employee, with whom I am obliged to deal, really inquire (alleging federal regulation) what I intend to do with the money I have withdrawn, or press me in a futile attempt to learn who my stockbroker is? No one would have asked that of my grandfather. (Ah, the employee wants me to invest with him;

that is, he seeks to take advantage of someone he views as a feeble woman of years.) Time was, within current memory, when those asking impertinent questions were sent away, sometimes with a shotgun, at least with authority that could not be challenged successfully. Nor did we trumpet on the rooftops our business. When Billie Holiday sang "Ain't Nobody's Business," and Hank Williams could advise someone that "if you mind your business, then you won't be mindin' mine," we all understood.

Picture the newly arrived freshman, not quite 17 at the time, at a prestigious college in Ohio, who had moved into her dorm room and was visited, on the pretext of "orientation," by a resident advisor (an upper-class student acting for the administration). Among other questions, the RA asks, "Have you had your lesbian experience yet?" Now, her parents, very liberal but not morally obtuse, were astounded and dismayed to learn of such an inquiry. The girl subsequently transferred to a university in Georgia. (I do not believe, though, that all the other freshmen so interrogated left that college; more's the pity.) She herself had not abdicated her privacy rights, of course; that had been done for her, by college authorities and their RA minions, and, behind them, American society as a whole, where such topics have become common themes for discussion in "group therapy" and college classes (sociology, psychology, and women's studies) and where social redesign *via* mind control is almost an official policy, nay, sometimes so stated. Dr. Freud is behind this in considerable part, but also the social engineers, who think, rightly, that making over the individual human being in his core relationships with others is the most direct and thorough way to reorder society.

Worse is the voluntary exposing of oneself—what shred may remain—and the dismantling of self-respect *via* what is almost an exhibitionist means: "social networking." I do wonder, by the way, how the chief perpetrator of the most successful of these networks had so much time on his hands while he was at Harvard. He is, we know, one Mark Zuckerberg, whose story inspired a film as well as a long *New Yorker* profile, who was *Time*'s 2010 Man of the Year (sorry, no, that's Person), and who has made billions and given some of them to the broken Newark, New Jersey, schools—as though huge amounts of money could remedy deep flaws in civil character and pedagogical practice. (It is acknowledged now that much was wasted.) "O Harvard, what crimes are committed in thy name!" Shouldn't he have been occupied instead with studying for, say, his advanced chemistry course, or classes in ancient or modern history, botany, foreign language, mathematics, English literature, philosophy, diplomacy and government?

Having hundreds of "friends" on a social site is preposterous; what can friendship (which the ancients valued highly) mean when it is so debased?

In apartment complexes, people often do not know the names, or recognize the faces, of their neighbors, but they have innumerable connections on Facebook! That won't help you much when you need a friend next door. Robert D. Putnam, a Harvard political scientist, suggested in his *Bowling Alone* (2000) that digital communication could not reverse what we now see as a loss of community skills. Similarly, in *Alone Together* (2011), Sherry Turtkle, a psychologist at MIT, expresses the opinion that technology is simultaneously interfering with our relationships with others and preventing us from knowing how to be alone.

Moreover, why would a sane person wish to share . . . well, I don't quite know what people put out for the more than one billion Facebook members, since I'm not one, but I believe they tell who they are (or what they think they are), what they did recently or intend to do, whom they are dating, what movies or "music" they like, whether they feel what they call "suicidal," and so on. Why should anyone proclaim abroad his daily habits, political views, or feelings of depression, or (more dangerously) his or her sexual preferences? Promiscuity is always bad. In this nation of 320 million inhabitants (or more), there are enormous numbers of cranks, and some are criminal and dangerous. By putting out photos of yourself and disseminating information—address and phone numbers, age, tastes, habits, means, family, and so on—you may meet one of those weirdos, or more than one. Anyhow, why should an adult get drawn into something designed by a Harvard student for his and his peers' amusement? (True, most of those in their 20's and 30's are adults only in name.) It is possible, to be sure, to put information on these sites to valid use; someone has suggested calling them "utilities," like power and telephone companies. That is not their main application, I fear.

The worst is that subscribers to Facebook and other sites become creatures of the network—that is, of others. "I exist because I am on Facebook and have given myself over to others' images of me." Tennyson could safely have his Ulysses proclaim, "I am a part of all that I have seen"; but I cannot imagine him, if he were alive, or even Lord Byron, subordinating his ego to Facebook. The noxious influence exerted through the "virtual presence" in one's life of hundreds, mostly unknowns, is incalculable. Think of what abuses can be wrought, intentionally or not, on those with weak character by fellow networkers, who can influence which films their correspondents choose to see, which songs they download, what improper language they use, even what they do and believe, in a serial relationship by which responsibility (or authority) is passed on and ultimately dissolved in an untraceable skein. At the same time these subscribers are subject to endless advertising, which pays for the experience. Is one to become a plaything of advertisers as well as one's "friends"?

The creature of the site and of other serial relationships is not Everyman, but No Man—belonging to all, hence belonging to none and particularly not himself. Such sites bear out *ipso facto* how today's egos, apparently so delicate, so starved for attention (their self-image gland having been enlarged to goiter proportions by schools and others), must find themselves by reflection through others, in a human hall of mirrors. Not only are countless hours wasted on social sites (as attested by confessed addicts—have they nothing else to do?); the person is dissipated, in a centrifugal movement. Human value cannot arise from technique, nor from social organization, even a good one; both are necessary but subordinate.

Georges Bernanos wrote more than once of the unspeakable crime of leading children astray. Even the doctor in *Diary of a Country Priest*, who has no religion, condemns those who would corrupt a child. Imagine a child of yours, 10 or 15 years old. You and others foster this child's good moral and intellectual growth, encourage and guide the child, giving examples by speech and action. Then the child gets a Facebook account, and all you have done may be blown away like dandelion fuzz.

This is very *soviétique.* Privacy under the Soviet regime, especially in the early decades, was generally unavailable; it was viewed as subversive. Though certain figures in power maintained it, the personal was looked at puritanically: something to be denounced and rooted out. It is not coincidental that families were broken up and children taken away. Widely disseminated propaganda supported the policy. The sexual interrogation alluded to above—or any sexual question posed by representatives of authority—is part of a social and political reconstruction project by which we will become "transparent" (one of Sartre's visions), with no inside, and thus, diffused like a fog, belong to the state or world community, a "global village" (when we have no decent village life here). Pride—not hubris nor the arrogance condemned by Scripture and displayed by our political figures, but self-respect with its sense of proper limits—will become obsolete.

Ultimately, privacy is connected to freedom—the freedom to be oneself, *not* to be transparent and the toy or product of others. The Soviet attitude toward privacy was directly related to its suppression of personal liberty, including moral and religious freedom. For the Soviets and their like, being in a society meant belonging wholly to that social environment. As Emmanuel Mounier, who founded a philosophy called *personnalisme*, wrote, "Man reduced to his social function is a cog-wheel."

The Uses of a Liberal Education

On September 1, 1939, an Englishman named Harry Hinsley, walking between two lines of Nazi soldiers, crossed slowly and nervously the bridge connecting Kehl in Germany with Strasbourg in France. He made it to the French side before the border was closed. He had been warned to leave. It was none too soon; German troops had already invaded Poland, and Great Britain declared war on Germany on September 3. Hinsley, an undergraduate at Cambridge, had spent his summer vacation across the Rhine learning some German. His field of study at Cambridge was medieval history; he worked on charts and other documents. What does one do with a history degree? Take up a teaching post immediately, or stay and get a postgraduate degree and *then* go teach, or remain forever within the college walls? Or seek other career opportunities—scholarly editing, publishing, museum or library work, a life in the clergy?

Hinsley did not yet need to choose. That autumn, he was interviewed and hired by representatives of what became Bletchley Park—the headquarters of the Government Code and Cipher School operations. He was only 20 years old. Some of his fellows in the campaign to break Germany's Enigma codes were similarly young: an Oxford mathematics graduate named Peter Twinn, aged 23, and an 18-year-old, Richard Pendered, who, after studies at Winchester, had been about to enroll at Cambridge. While Hinsley (who after the war returned to St. John's College as an historian) was helped by these two students of mathematics and others, it was he who masterminded the codebreaking operation by means of reconstructing the German codes.

Among the older staff members at Bletchley Park was an eccentric former classical scholar, "Dilly" Knox, who likewise knew German and who liked poetry—while driving, he would recite Milton's "Lycidas." Now, how could acquaintance with poetry possibly be of any use? Well, during the previous war, in 1917, when he was at work on the naval flag code used by the Germans, he recognized that a piece of code was the enciphered version of a poem by Friedrich Schiller, which then served as a crib. At Bletchley Park there was also Mavis Lever, who at age 18 had interrupted her study of German at London University; she did not work on German, however, but on Italian Naval Enigma, which she was instrumental in breaking. The work of these cryptographers and others doubtless shortened the 1939-45 war, eased conditions during its course in Britain and elsewhere (by helping protect merchant shipping in the Atlantic), and saved countless lives.

The uses to which any education can be put are, clearly, a function of what that education is. (Hence remarks below on what it should not be.) With the mind as both tool and target, a true liberal-arts education allows us to *go beyond* what we know and what we are. If well taught, history (often deemed useless), languages (studied too much as a traveler's aid), good literary prose (not today's degraded fiction and propaganda), poetry, sound philosophy, including political philosophy, mathematics and the mathematics-based sciences—all these *develop the mind* in reasoning, memory, knowledge, powers of assessment and reflection, and imagination. They prepare the learner to confront material, systematic or otherwise, that, at the outset, is unfamiliar, perhaps recalcitrant. A good poem, for example, which is a small, detailed system, the principles of which may be obvious (rhyme scheme, meter, stanzas) or less so (metaphors, subtle references, interior echoes, a kind of poetic "argument"), invites analysis as a means of appreciation. The Bletchley Park staff members had native intelligence but also solid and broad training in one or more fields of the liberal arts and sciences—that is to say, in learning, thinking, and then applying their powers of thought. They knew how to reason, hence guess at others' reasoning, how to see both detail and outline, assess a field, and imagine solutions. They could harness language for their purposes. They had learned *how to learn.*

In other words, as the French novelist Butor observed about his literary endeavors, a genuine liberal education makes you *more intelligent.* A mental Sisyphus, you develop the muscles of your mind, which, flexible and provided with a wide range of knowledge, can think, invent, and tackle a variety of challenges and puzzles, including entirely novel ones that arise in new fields or undertakings. How many of today's students, often committed early to vocational subjects such as business and finance or a program of fluff (so-called communication, sociology, or gender or ethnic studies, for instance), will remain for the next four or five decades in the occupational field for which these studies have, in fact or purportedly, prepared them? Many will be obliged to switch careers or face redesigned jobs, with consequent loss of time, income, often contentment. Yet students and their parents commonly believe they should study little except what will allow them to get certified as soon as possible to work in a practical field. This is a narrow view; it would be more useful to prepare mentally for almost inevitable changes and disruptions. Even medicine and law will continue to change: medicine (under great political and economic pressures right now) through scientific discoveries, applied ingenuity, modified attitudes and policies, different organizational arrangements, and altered insurance schemes; law by new legislation, constant legal challenges, foreign influences (probably), and the reinterpretation of constitutions and statutes. Knox, Hinsley, Lever, and various mathematicians at Bletchley had no idea, during their studies, to what use their mental skills and knowledge would be put.

Liberal studies have, in short, a civic and cultural use and a practical one, the two often intertwined. If properly defined and well carried out, by responsible and well-grounded teachers, liberal studies free students from mental parochialism and dangerous illusions—ignorance, foolishness, and false idols—and prepare them to live intelligently and responsibly. We, like the British then and now, are in great need of well-trained minds and critical abilities (and courageous hearts), since the enemies are not only at our borders but within. We should beware, however, of educational rhetoric today (in college propaganda materials, for instance) that speaks of "developing critical thinking." In the new coded language, *critical* has come to mean hostile "deconstruction" of Occidental culture, institutions, and thought, especially white "patriarchy," the colonialist mentality, and traditional views on sex. The enthusiasts of "critical thinking" are, in fact, weak in critical faculties, as a perusal of their writings would show.

When the components of a liberal curriculum are watered down or not approached rigorously and objective elements are not stressed, the mind achieves little and is often warped and lured into a false appraisal of its capacities. The unfortunate trend today is away from "judgmental" assessments and toward indiscriminate acceptance of everything—everything, that is, except what the purveyors of political correctness do not like. In the milieu that Jonathan M. Smith and Jim Norwine, two antirevisionist geographers writing in *Academic Questions* (Fall 2009), call "the bawdy saloon of progressive politics, cultural nihilism, and subjective epistemology," so-called education is downright dangerous for students and poisonous for society (though profitable for its purveyors). If we teach the view of minimalist sculptor Donald Judd (who disfigured some fine desert landscape in Presidio County, Texas, with his huge horrors), to wit, "If you call it art, it *is* art," the only result will be degraded taste and judgment, made notorious by the buzz of scandal and transgression. Think of the late Mr. Mapplethorpe. A more obscure illustration has been furnished by composer Heinz Holliger, whose "Ostinato funèbre" includes sounds of tearing paper, pouring water, and crunching twigs.

The "bawdy saloon" is what a good liberal education is *not*. Alas, classroom work and writing in the humanities and social sciences at the college level (and, it appears, in secondary schools also) have become chiefly a matter of expressing one's opinion—first by the instructors, then by the students. Opinions teach little or nothing and can be pernicious. Though students believe they think for themselves, they are, in fact, often docile—more so than those of the Eisenhower decade, who are despised—and are content to regurgitate platitudes and instructors' cherished points of view, usually mindlessly liberal, or simply assert their own, derivative ones, demonstrating that they belong to what Harold Rosenberg called "the herd of independent minds." "Question Authority," says a bumper sticker. Whose authority—that of those despised by the bumper-sticker writer, or perhaps of the one who devised the sticker? Youth duped by this precept—half-victims, half-accomplices—assail traditions of patriotism and family, for instance, but eagerly swallow a whole stinking stew of ravings by an unkempt neo-Marxist. The reduction in core requirements favors this trend. Not long ago the University of Arkansas reduced its general-education demands for the B.A. from 66 hours to 35, eliminating foreign-language requirements and watering down science. Bowdoin College has seen to it that students have *no* field or subject requirements. Others have followed suit. Or if there is a requirement, it is a "service course," in which students are obliged to work for a progressive cause ("sustainability," for instance).

Subjectivity, thus ease, is all. Says the student who has been exposed to *Beloved* in three or four courses, "I just feel that Morrison is a great writer." There is scarcely any understanding that literary and artistic judgment, not to mention moral judgment, must be founded in order to be sound and persuasive; otherwise there is no judgment—there are merely imitative, tropistic reactions, with a usual preference for what is base. If feeling is to be part of judgment—and there is no implication here that emotion should be removed from the range of legitimate human responses—it too must be properly understood and justified, not the brute reaction of an impulsive, silly biped.

Cultivation of self-image is another unfortunate major strain in humanities courses (hence the enormous popularity of creative-writing curricula). A philosophy professor of my acquaintance taught yearly "The Philosophy of Self." Consisting greatly, I think, of star-gazing at the contemporary "self," and padded with "discussions," it had a very large enrollment, much larger than the courses on Plato and Aristotle given by a scholar and teacher of excellent reputation in the same institution. Such self-cultivation is, by and large, useless at best or, worse, a harmful indulgence; it certainly is not mind-training. Similarly, in the social sciences and especially "feel-good" and multicultural studies, *a priori* suppositions, clichés, and shibboleths rule. As for such abominations as "feminist mathematics," no comment is necessary. As part of this trend, standards of grading, it is well known, have been lowered and requirements eased; liberal-arts studies are no longer the touchstone they should be. "I just feel that Proust is too hard and we should not have to read all this." Some years ago it was reported that at Duke University, one of the hotbeds of postmodernist brainwashing, more than 60 percent of the students graduated with honors. What an extraordinary group of human beings! Soon everyone will graduate at the top of his class and be equally certified. That may be all right in rubbish such as gender studies; I wouldn't like it, say, in ophthalmological surgery or suspension-bridge design.

A proper liberal-arts education is, to be sure, an expensive enterprise—for *someone*—students, parents, state, philanthropists, society as a whole. (That is, unless, as well may be the case, it is the result of self-teaching—reading, reflection, short courses, exchanges with others. Autodidactic training is now better than much of what can be purchased. In a *New York Times* article, Jacques Steinberg even proposed, as his title put it, "Plan B: Skip College.") Four expensive years, even devoted to top-notch learning, with little to show except mental agility and awareness—quite some holiday, right? What, however, is the social and political price of ignorance, blindness, incompetence, and the total neglect of our patrimony? We observe today the consequences of this neglect.

It might be objected that, if the entire college population studied nothing but ancient philosophy, medieval history, English poetry, astronomy, and so on, there would be insufficient numbers of technicians, managers, and others to run the country. Ah, but if the college population were reduced to what it should be—those who really want higher learning, not just a certificate to open a career door—then society could easily afford to provide the sort of education sketched out here and would be better off for it; as my argument goes, these educated people would in many cases become better technicians and managers than those ostensibly trained for such posts. If in fact nearly all those aged 18 were to attend college, as Presidents Clinton and Obama have wished, at least they could be obliged to take courses in ethics (and not designed by the NEA or NOW).

As the earlier examples show, society is served by the development of minds and mastery of liberal branches of knowledge; national survival may depend on such training applied to civic service. For most of us, however, it is impossible, despite our training, to contribute much to this nation, which groans under a combination of atomized machine and mob rule and oligarchic control—and presently suffers, as Tom Piatak and numerous others have pointed out, from the negative effects of globalization. The ancient ideals and modes of civic life on which our republic was founded have been so abandoned or crushed, and the economic system so altered, that few of us can, as the expression goes, "make a difference."

Individuals, thus, may be the greater beneficiaries of genuine liberal education. What we can do with our learning is live well for ourselves, our families, like-minded people in our circles, and those whose welfare may be partly in our hands. To say that may beg the question; for what is living well? Merely a personal choice, some would argue; one may choose to watch a monster-truck derby, attend cult gatherings, or use "recreational" drugs in the evening, or, in contrast, meet intelligent, charming friends for dinner ("Conversation forms the mind," wrote Pascal), or visit a worthwhile art or science exhibit, spend time with our children, listen to music, or read the classics, history, and good contemporary books. As Henry David Thoreau asserted in "Reading," "Books are the treasured wealth of the world, and the fit inheritance of generations and nations. Books stand naturally and rightfully on the shelves of every cottage." William Chase echoed him not long ago: "Knowledge of those books [standard literary works] and the tradition in which they exist is a human good in and of itself." The whole point of the learning promoted here is that it enables us to go beyond indiscriminate choices in a life that is "nasty, brutish, and short" (think of young Hollywood "celebrities" recently deceased) and distinguish the good from the less good—then share this understanding and its fruits with others. Dilly Knox of Bletchley Park had liked Schiller's and Milton's poetry for its own sake—that is, for what it offered to his mind and heart. (It will be recalled that Stevens observed, "The pleasure of poetry is to contribute to man's happiness.") It was almost serendipitous that Knox could use his acquaintance with poetry to break a code. *Almost* serendipitous, but not entirely, because poetry had afforded training as well as pleasure—the sort of training that allowed him to identify a clue.

With luck and prudence, one's mind lasts as long as one's life, and a true education can provide decades-long satisfaction through understanding, wisdom, and intellectual and aesthetic pleasure. The cultivation of one's garden is the cultivation of oneself, and, more broadly, the defense of civilization. What will our fellow countrymen do with themselves in a future time of leisure, or, like Dante, in exile? Watch reality shows or play video games? After he retired, my grandfather (as my readers know) collected and enjoyed books, traveled, listened to recorded music on his Zenith phonograph, and wrote for the next 24 years. His previous endeavors as an humane scientist, researcher, and lover of knowledge had not only rewarded him as he served others but prepared him wonderfully for his old age.

These observations do not fall here upon deaf ears. I am preaching to the converted, except for a very few, who may have come to scoff but "remain'd to pray." What I should like is for readers to reflect on these matters additionally and share their views with others in their circles; then, if circumstances allow, to make these arguments in print and before school boards, university trustees (when universities beg for money), legislatures, and others in power, and thus to prove me partially wrong about "making a difference."

Islands of Our Years

OF THE PATTERNS AND METAPHORS by which we perceive, measure, and relate our lives, one of the oldest and most insistent is that of the journey. Shakespeare uses the sea voyage image frequently, as in *Julius Caesar*:

> There is a tide in the affairs of men,
> Which, taken at the flood, leads on to fortune;
> Omitted, all the voyage of their life
> Is bound in shallows and in miseries.

Expressions such as "travel life's road" and "along our way" are stock elements of graduation ceremonies, sermons, and greeting cards; such words are spoken at weddings and murmured at funerals. The literary-minded think back to the wanderings of Odysseus and those of Aeneas; they think of knights errant and the *matière de Bretagne*; they know that the picaresque novel arose out of such romances and adventure stories, and that numerous outstanding English novels are quasi-epics (*The Adventures of Tom Jones*, for instance), in the plots of which journeys and digressions from the journey play a significant role. One of these masterpieces features a real voyage over perilous seas by "an everyman," as J. Paul Hunter called Robinson Crusoe, "a wanderer on a sea he does not understand," who is marooned for 28 years—a story based perhaps on the real case of Alexander Selkirk and his island to the west of Chile.

If life can be thus felt, according to the pattern set by Odysseus in the "mid-earth sea," as travel through space and time, especially as a sea voyage (with the related metaphors of ports, storms, rocks and eddies, wreckage), then it is also strung with islands—those clusters of years, activities, associates that rise above the horizon and constitute stopping-places, places of relief, of discovery sometimes, perhaps of danger. Literature is full of such islands. Shakespeare needed an isle (inspired by Bermuda, some believe) as the setting for *The Tempest*. Think too of *Treasure Island*, which has haunted boys' imaginations since 1883; think of *The Count of Monte Cristo* and the two islands that play a role in the adventure of Dantès, first the Château d'If (the prison island), then the place of treasure, to which l'abbé Faria directs him. In American writing, there is scarcely any place more fundamental than the island in the Mississippi on which Huck Finn and Jim find themselves.

More broadly the cities of civilization are islands, so to speak, some of them literally—"the isles of Greece! the isles of Greece!" (Byron) and Sicily. I think also of the oases of the Near East—gardens of art, science, and language surrounded by sand and desolation. Perhaps, on the other side of the world, the South Pacific islands should be mentioned, from which men in outriggers or canoes set sail, or drifted, to the east and the other hemisphere, where eventually they established pre-Columbian civilizations. The earth itself is a kind of isle in the universe, surrounded by waves of time and space, "islanded in its stream of stars," as Henry Beston wrote. Astronauts have remarked on its singular blue beauty. Like Saint-Exupéry's Little Prince, we are travelers, fallen from the skies, finding a home on our cosmic isle.

Or are we ourselves unmoored islands, floating masses of stuff, half-directed by oar or rudder, half-driven by the winds of fate and the dark, unseen currents below? "No man is an island," said John Donne; but Arnold, for whom "the sea of faith" had ebbed, wrote:

> Yes! In the sea of life enisled,
> With echoing straits between us thrown,
> Dotting the shoreless watery wild,
> We mortals live *alone* . . .

Though Arnold spoke in moral and metaphysical terms—terms we would call existential, stressing the death of God and forlorn condition of man—rather than from the sociological perspective of this new millennium, we can apply his insight likewise to the atomization of society (and its components, including in extreme cases the very self) or, rather, *societies*, as formerly constituted—that is, culturally coherent polities.

Among the earliest of such polities were those Greek city-states to which citizens belonged (Aristotle wrote that a citizen is one who has a share in judging and ruling); later, despite conflicts among them, Italian city-states and the free cities of Europe, then the early nation-states, as well as the whole of Christendom, constituted, in the Occident, such coherent and embracing polities. These units were not, however, without contacts in the wider world; the "echoing straits" could be crossed. Even the larger nation-states of the modern period—Great Britain, France, other European empires or monarchies, and the early United States—had political and social coherence.

Now we are supposed to be a "global culture." There are 320 million individuals in this country alone and some seven billion on the planet. If one believes sociologists and similar commentators, the more numerous we are, the more solitary we feel and the more solipsistically we act: hence the need for hundreds of "friends" on Facebook. How faithful these "friends" are to one another (as Arnold asked that lovers be true on the darkling plain) is unclear.

Since I was a girl, I have been drawn to islands of any size. Low sandbars in the Platte River in Colorado; little clumps of sandy or boggy soil covered with willows where we could fish, in the Rio Grande or the Gunnison River; Padre Island, off the coast of south Texas, which I saw at age ten; countless others, including the barrier islands off the Atlantic coast and the northern Gulf of Mexico, with their dunes and sea oats. Recently, as Patric and I drove along U.S. Highway 40 beside the Colorado River in Grand County, west of the Continental Divide, I admired in the streambed fine islets dotted with cottonwood trees, willows, and some conifers—beckoning to us, as it were. I could imagine, were I there, feeling the world flowing by. But the image is not unambiguous. I am reminded of optical tests concerning ground and subject, and the paintings of Maurits Escher: Does one see water against a background of land, or land against water? Which is our true milieu? One of the ironies of sea islands is the frequent absence of fresh water. What should be a refuge from, say, storm or shipwreck (or the madding crowd) may be close to uninhabitable. We must suppose that when Saint John, called the Divine, repaired to the island of Patmos, he found at least the bare necessities to sustain his visions.

Other travelers may have seen many more archipelagos and other islands than I, and more exotic ones, such as the Seychelles; but I delight at least in thoughts of those distant ones I have visited and often written about: the Alexander Archipelago off the coast of Alaska, the Inner Hebrides, the West Indies, including the U.S. Virgin Islands, and, above all, Sicily. While, since his poetry is powerfully magnetizing, my devotion to the writing of Saint-John Perse (who used his birth name, Alexis Saint-Leger Leger, in his private life and diplomatic career) does not depend upon his being, like me, born and reared in the Western Hemisphere (on his family's island and then Guadeloupe proper), surely his tie to the islands of the Caribbean, and his evocation of them in a French both precise and tinged with the marvelous, help connect his sensibility to mine. His first published series of poems is called *Images à Crusoé*.

Part of my love of islands is the taste for solitude. Don't we all wish to be left alone?—except, of course, when we want others, and then we hope, or even expect, that they will be ready to see us, hear us, help us, giving up their own occupations because we are available once again and need them. As Anne Morrow Lindbergh observed with regret, thinking of the responsibilities and complications of her life and her need for refuge, one cannot permanently inhabit a desert island. Another strain in my liking for islands is the love of simplicity, both a moral and an aesthetic virtue. To be sure, in art, the elaborate deserves our homage—as in Notre-Dame de Paris, Beauvais, and Chartres, Yorkminster, and the basilica of Vézelay, not to mention great baroque edifices in Germany, Italy, and Austria, such as the Melk Abbey, on the Danube. Where, however, do the penitent, the petitioner go? To the side chapel, where grace seems nearer than in the nave, the way to God more direct.

Similarly, musical creations of tremendous development and complexity, such as some by Bach, inspire awe. Yet Wolfgang Amadeus Mozart's "Ave verum corpus," with its 46 measures and its pure phrasing, is fully as moving. In philosophy the most elaborate systems, albeit remarkable edifices of the mind, have little bearing on our own lives and beliefs; who really lives by Immanuel Kant, or Arthur Schopenhauer, or Martin Heidegger? Not that they have no value for reflection; they can, we presume, broaden our grasp of ideas and develop reasoning ability. How profound the human understanding derived from them may be, I cannot say.

Despite dreaming of an island retreat, I do not feel myself cut off, in Arnold's sense or others, an unconnected, unloved being, in meaningless anomie; but I easily conceive of places and experiences as standing out against the flow of things on the sea of life, or, like the "islands" of Louisiana topography—pine or cypress groves or salt domes—rising above the mainly undifferentiated landscape of marsh, prairie, and cane fields. (In mid- and late-18th century treaties New Orleans itself was called the "Isle of Orleans," bounded by the Mississippi River, the small Manchac River, Lakes Maurepas and Pontchartrain to the north, and Lake Borgne; as such, it was exempted from the territory of "West Florida," transferred back and forth.)

Wasn't the little town of Alpine something of an island for my family in the wilds of West Texas? More an oasis, of course; and it admitted some strange travelers, with few questions asked by the local citizenry. But, if one pictures the surrounding Chihuahua desert, its dunes and arroyos, its mountain crests, as a waving, billowing ocean, then it is easy to see how the feeling of island could be strong, as in any small, isolated community. Trees had been planted and watered, churches built, a little college established, and the simple customs and connections of human beings had a local habitation in which to flourish. My father and mother were not the least of those who contributed neighborly acts, learning, integrity, and moral distinction.

I could not return to that oasis to stay. In 2005, however, a friend and I drove there from her home in Austin. Though a Texas native, she had never visited the Big Bend. Whether she liked it I cannot say; she is not fond of dry open spaces, I believe, having been reared and nearly blown away in the

Panhandle. We stopped in Ft. Davis, stayed two nights in an Alpine motel, and visited the courthouse and the cemetery, with my parents' graves and those of various friends. I had told my friend that I did not want to see my parents' house; the previous time I'd driven by, years before, the sight was too painful—my keen memories of contentment and loss were poisoned by the deteriorated property. Instead she and I stopped on a side street, and she walked around to take photographs. When I looked at the snapshots later, I was not, in fact, too distressed, but that was because of the screen of trees, which had grown and branched out well from their humble beginnings in the 1950's as seedlings from a catalog. We also drove to Marfa, 26 miles away, where, as always, I admired the old Paisano Hotel, still open and actually receiving tourists! That town has become, inexplicably, an arty, trendy place. Ah, there is such a thing as too much money, with too little taste. The semi-idle youth constitute the new leisure class, with their bars and bands and six-year college sojourns.

For me school was never an island; it was the current, the Gulf Stream of my life. From age five until I retired, I spent most of every year at some sort of educational establishment, and, in professorial days, doing research and writing books were part of my schoolwork even in the summer. As far as that goes, I haven't left the campus yet, in every way; I frequent libraries and pursue my scholarship in the manner of Dr. Johnson's harmless drudge. True, in this stream of learning, as in the Sargasso Sea, there are identifiable clusters distinct from the rest of the course, which provided unusual meaning of various sorts; there were even islands, as for Odysseus, lit now brightly in my memory (but without the danger). Rice University, for some years; France, for a Fulbright year; various early teaching positions. But the current flowed, and when I reached Tulane and stayed there for 29 years (with some months away for short-term professorships in Canada and England), I was not becalmed, but felt a smooth, steady undercurrent.

My marriage to Paul Brosman, now deceased, was not an island, neither fertile nor deserted. Instead, it ran parallel to the stream of the university—not identical, and not so smooth a course (there were many squalls), but, like it, part of the mainstream of my middle years. The birth of our daughter created a third current in that stream, one of growth and development and enormous lasting satisfaction. "Who would fardels bear?" asks Hamlet. Many of us do, for the sake of one person or more, one vocation, one cause or another. Now, however, that I am remarried to Patric, my first husband, I can see marriage to Paul as a long interval—even perhaps a dead calm, without the calm—a time that tries one's mettle, and thus is "a precious jewel" like that of the toad, which builds character. Similarly Patric's long years of marriage to another woman cannot be viewed as an island. It was his mainstream, along with his profession—the locus, reason, and shape of what he did; it helped define him and furnish the very feeling of his existence. Yet in those decades he was adrift, not professionally, but without the fulfillment that a good marriage should bring. Now, together, we have reached the island of our age, green, even lush with love regained.

I wonder whether the very souls of men should be imagined as islands—apparently disconnected from the great continents of spirit that may be around us, yet joined at a deep level, the equivalent of the sea floor. We know that our minds, being both held (enclosed in their cranium, in the world) and holding (containing what contains them—as though they had been turned inside out), reach out to other minds and, through direct and symbolic means, conceive the whole earth and universe or at least what is now known about them. There is no end to speculation. Didn't Stevens write that "The Palm at the end of the mind / Beyond the last thought, rises"? John Greenleaf Whittier even conceived of God's isles floating in eternity, a tropical archipelago, fresh with mercy:

I know not where His islands lift
Their fronded palms in air;
I only know I cannot drift
Beyond His love and care.

Who knows what waves out there in space and time will carry us, or be carried to us, by the currents of the cosmos?

"*Grand âge, nous voici*," wrote Saint-John Perse. Patric and I have passed between Scylla and Charybdis; plugging our ears or tying ourselves to the mast, we've heard and survived the Sirens' singing; we've visited lotus eaters, the Cyclops' cave and other kingdoms of the monstrous, one-eyed (the meaner for it) or blind—or maybe we two were the blind ones. We've even had moments in Hades, hoping to find the dead, wishing to offer sacrifice. We took care of those who depended on us. (Hell, said Bernanos, is to love no longer.) Perhaps our sacrifices were accepted. "*Heureux qui comme Ulysse a fait un long voyage*," said the Renaissance poet Joachim Du Bellay, whose Odysseus finally arrives home to live "*le reste de son âge*."

Islands in space, islands in time—we have kept many good memories of them and retained lessons taught. We have stripped down to something like the simplicity and self-containment of isles seen against vast waters; we learned to shape space and create points of happiness. We have continuity but not continuousness. Much of the time we live plainly (though not ascetically), indulging ourselves on other occasions by opera and ballet performances, book collecting, travel, and time with friends. The rich joys of literature are always there. We're not cocooned, though; human solidarity demands recognition of the disasters and threats around us, notwithstanding our inability to improve matters in the least. We will watch the intermittences of days and tides come and go. By the grace of age and love, on this last island of our particular journey, we will drink from the freshets of experience, admire the palms, and look for pearly oysters in coves and bottled messages on the sands of the day.

Notes

While complete documentation for every quotation and reference in the text is not given here, the sources of selected passages are provided.

Preface. The quotation comes from a brief anonymous review of Paul Auster's *Winter Journal* (Holt), which appeared in *The New Yorker*, 3 Sept. 2012.

"Music From the Lake." The quotation from *First Things* is from the October 2011 issue. The comment on absence of constraint in the 1970's was made by Nathan Heller in *The New Yorker*, 24 Oct. 2011.

"Generations." Rhodes's view of race is mentioned by Clifford Sharp in his essay on Rhodes in H.J. Massingham and Hugh Massingham, eds., *The Great Victorians* (London: Ivor Nicholson & Watson, 1932), 430. I wish to thank Dr. Jeannine Hayat, whose reflections on this topic in the context of her teaching at the Lycée Racine in Paris led me to compose this essay.

"*The New Yorker* Under the Glass." The statements from Jenny Diski are from the issue of 26 Sept. 2011. The quotations from James Wood come from "Off the Map" in the issue of 23 January 2012. The Pittsburgh author is Sheryl St. Germain.

"In the Abbey." The poem in question, "In the Abbaye d'Ardenne," is in my collection *Places in Mind* (2000).

"How the Historical Novel Has Changed!" Rice's statement is quoted by Jack Trotter in his "Unreal Bodies, Unholy Blood," *Chronicles: A Magazine of American Culture*, October 2011.

"Four Modes of Book Collecting." The report about Longfellow is often quoted; one source is Charles C. Calhoun, *Longfellow: A Rediscovered Life* (Boston: Beacon Press, 2004). James Wood's assertion comes from *The New Yorker*, 7 November 2011. The quotation from Eugene

Field comes from his *The Love Affairs of a Bibliomaniac* (New York: Scribner's, 1896), vi.

"In Defense of Poesie." The quotation on art and matter in poetry can be found in Lascelles Abercrombie, in Massingham and Massingham, 88.

"Adventures With Food." The article on Uchi was published in the *Houston Chronicle*, 8 Feb. 2012. The term "gastronauts" and the spelling "Eataly" were used by Andrei Navrazov in "Eating Cake," *Chronicles: A Magazine of American Culture*, June 2012. On the Haiti earthquake aftermath and stealing, see "Running in the Ruins," *The New Yorker*, 6 Sept. 2010. On failures of humanitarian aid abroad generally, see "Alms Dealers," *The New Yorker*, 11 October 2010. Gide's statement comes from *Ainsi soit-il, ou les jeux sont faits* (Paris: Gallimard, 1952), 23. The quotation on dismissing the cook comes from Alphonse Julien, *Richard Wagner* (1892; trans. Florence Percival Hall, rpt. Neptune, NJ: Paganiniana Publications, 1981), 177. Haley's statement was published in *Chronicles: A Magazine of American Culture*, May 2012.

"Secure of Private Right." The quotation comes from Keizer's book *Privacy* (2012). A cofounder of Facebook was Chris Hughes, who helped manage Obama's web strategy in 2008.

"The Uses of a Liberal Education." Tom Piatak's opinion is expressed in "Bringing Back the Old Economy," *Chronicles: A Magazine of American Culture*, April 2010. The Chase quotation comes from *The American Scholar*, Autumn 2009.

About the Author

Catharine Savage Brosman, a poet, essayist, and scholar, is Professor Emerita of French at Tulane University and Honorary Research Professor at the University of Sheffield, where she held the De Velling & Willis Visiting Professorship for a term. She serves as poetry editor of *Chronicles: A Magazine of American Culture.* At Tulane she was Mellon Professor of Humanities in 1990 and later held the Gore Chair in French. After nearly 40 years in New Orleans, she settled in Houston in 2007. She and her husband spend their summers in Colorado, her native state. Poems of hers have appeared all over the U.S. and in England and France, and she has published ten collections, with a new one in press for 2017. In addition, her poetry has been anthologized frequently and featured on the radio and on internet sites such as Poetry Daily and American Life in Poetry. Dr. Brosman's previous collections of personal and cultural essays are *The Shimmering Maya and Other Essays* (1994) and *Finding Higher Ground: A Life of Travels* (2003). Her scholarly publications comprise 18 volumes on French literary history and criticism and two on American literature: *Louisiana Creole Literature: A Historical Study* (2013) and *Southwestern Women Writers and the Vision of Goodness* (2016).

www.ingramcontent.com/pod-product-compliance
Lightning Source LLC
Chambersburg PA
CBHW030757150426
42813CB00068B/3186/J
* 9 7 8 1 9 4 3 2 1 8 0 2 8 *